STD/HIV
Prevention
Action

Let's Protect Each Other

Samuel Frimpong MD, MPH

iUniverse, Inc.
New York Bloomington

STD/HIV Prevention Action

Let's Protect Each Other

iUniverse books may be ordered through booksellers or by contacting:

iUniverse
1663 Liberty Drive
Bloomington, IN 47403
www.iuniverse.com
1-800-Authors (1-800-288-4677)

ISBN: 978-0-595-52137-1(sc)
ISBN: 978-0-595-62202-3 (ebook)
ISBN: 978-0-595-51135-8 (dj)

Printed in the United States of America

iUniverse rev. date: 01/18/2010

I take this opportunity to thank Pearson Education, Inc., for giving me permission to use illustrations of human reproductive systems from their book *Essentials of Human Anatomy and Physiology.*

Acknowledgments

I am grateful to my dear wife, son, and daughter for allowing me to use much of our family time to write this book.

I thank Patricia L. Pegues for compiling a file of pictures of sexually transmitted diseases (STDs) for me, which were used to add more meaning to some of the diseases, especially syphilis. To Joyce S. Anane and her daughter Alek S. Djokoto, thank you very much for your wisdom in helping to make the STD pictures a part of this book.

I want to acknowledge Marian Tabi, RN, PhD, MPH, Associate Professor of Nursing at Georgia Southern University, for taking time to review this book. Thanks to Tommy Chandler, BSc. of Duval County Health Department STD Field Operations Unit for sharing his forty-five years of STD intervention experience with me and encouraging me to write this book. I want to thank Lloyd Seaman, BA and Michael Guyton for the team work with Tommy Chandler. Together, you all have remarkable interest in field surveillance of syphilis and dedicated to control syphilis in Jacksonville (Duval County), Florida for the past thirty years. Also thanks to the entire staff especially Sharon Reiley D., RN, an STD nurse clinician, for numerous experiences we shared together to give our clients the chance to test and get treatment for syphilis, gonorrhea, chlamydia, and HIV.

I appreciate the zeal and the enthusiasm demonstrated by Danijela Causevic and Awah Fuamenya Ajoache, MPH, both disease intervention specialists (DIS) in the Duval County Health Department, for reading early drafts of the manuscript. I acknowledge the time spent by Patsy Walters and Elder Daniel Aboagye to read the manuscript.

My sincere thanks goes to George E. Nedeff for helping with editing, Liesl Schapker and Amy R. He and other staff members of iUniverse publishers for publishing this book.

Dedication

I dedicate this book to my dear uncle, the late Dr. E.O.A. Asibey, a former employee of the World Bank and author of the book title "My First Book of Mammals". He worked throughout his life to conserve animals and trees all over the world and was passionate about caring for people especially when they were sick. Dr. Asibey teamed up with my dear late Auntie Yaa Konadu and selflessly used part of their financial resources to encourage and help me to get the best education I could manage to get, to learn and apply medical knowledge to solve problems, and to take care of patients. Their wishes for me have been fulfilled, and I believe they will rest in peace.

Preface

Any time a person starts having sex with a wrong person without testing for STD/HIV, that person puts his or her life and safety on line for a reduced quality of life after HIV infection which has no cure. Many people are meeting wrong sex partners on web sites by the internet, and clubs, who use fake names and do not care about the sex partner except to have sex. Such anonymous wrong sex partners will refuse to get tested for STD/HIV and verify results before sex, keep their HIV status and where they live and their sexual lifestyle secret from the sex partner, may have many other sex partners and never ready to commit to only one sex partner. Anonymous wrong sex partners more often infect men who have sex with men (MSM) and women with STD/HIV. It is not money, the look of the person, the way the person talks or talent because none of those is worth more than anyone's life. Therefore, everybody must be careful, have a STD/HIV prevention action plan and stay alive.

CONTENTS

Introduction

Sexually transmitted diseases and HIV infections have affected millions of people throughout the world. When I came from Ghana, West Africa, to the United States as a legal immigrant to pursue a career in public health and internal medicine and then became a U.S. citizen, I found a nation that cares so much about the suffering of other nationalities all around the world and has been at the forefront of helping others in need. I realized then that I had begun a journey that would shape my life in helping others in need of disease prevention especially sexually transmitted diseases (STD) including human immunodeficiency virus (HIV) and acquired immunodeficiency syndrome (AIDS). I am indebted to others and wish to share my experience that I belief will help many people all around the world especially the youth and young adults in the age 15–24. My message to them is to protect themselves and others from STD/HIV infections and the associated complications of these diseases.

Thus, in the introduction of this book, let me tell you about the impact of STD/HIV on the lives of people especially young women and the socioeconomic burden of the STD/HIV epidemic beginning in the country of Ghana, where I was born, and moving to the United States of America where my values to help others to protect themselves from STD/HIV has evolved.

When I was growing up in Ghana, West Africa, as a child, I had a cousin who lived and ate together with me from the same household. Her father was the king of the town and was my father's senior brother. She and I started first grade together in the same elementary school, and we were in the same class until I left the senior high school to go to junior college. She was a king's daughter—a well-brought-up princess—and had everything she needed until she graduated from high school.

She left her father's house to live in the city with relatives and enjoyed an average life with friends and extended family members in the city of Kumasi, the capital of the Ashanti Region of Ghana. She began a relationship with a man and became pregnant, but the man did not marry her. During the subsequent years from 1981 to 1990 the economy of the country was not good. There was migration of Ghanaians to the countries of Nigeria and Cote d'Ivoire in West Africa. Both Nigeria and Cote d'Ivoire had a prosperous economy during that period of time due to a stable government and abundant natural and intellectual human resources.

The migrants to Cote d'Ivoire were mostly women who went to live in the capital, Abidjan, to trade and make friends and enjoy a city life. My dear cousin joined the train of migrant traders to Abidjan and left behind a baby boy in the care of her parents. Unfortunately, some of the women who traveled to Cote d'Ivoire including my cousin, the princess, returned to Ghana from 1988 to 1995 with HIV infection and died from AIDS.

I was a student at the University of Ghana Medical School in Accra, Ghana, when I heard that she had returned from Abidjan to Kumasi and died within a few days from the complications of AIDS. Her son had lost the chance to grow up with his mother because of her early death from a preventable STD called HIV/AIDS. I realized that I had missed the opportunity to share with her the knowledge I had acquired in medical school about STD/HIV infections. We had lost communication with each other from the time she had moved to Abidjan.

The Ghanaian economy has since improved over the past eight years due to a stable government. There is reduced migration to Cote d'Ivoire where the HIV rate is higher compared to Ghana. The HIV infection rates in Ghana have remained among the lowest in West Africa.

While I was in medical school and after graduation, I worked in obstetrics and gynecology and then in the internal medicine department of the Korle-bu teaching hospital in Accra, Ghana, where I had been trained as a medical officer. I came into contact with many young and beautiful women who could not naturally get pregnant. Most of them found out that their fallopian tubes were blocked because of late diagnosis and incomplete treatment of recurrent STDs such as chlamydia and gonorrhea.

During that period, in vitro fertilization was not part of infertility management in Ghana because of lack of facilities. Many of the women had no money to undergo further work up for infertility. The women had missed the opportunity to know and understand that regular testing for STD and annual Pap smears could have helped to diagnose

STDs early when they could benefit from early treatment. They had no knowledge that late diagnosis of STDs could rob them of the chance to get pregnant naturally and give birth to the children they desired.

I bore the pain of such women, especially those who were extended family members and family friends who got married and found out that they could not get pregnant because of fallopian tube blockage from STDs they acquired from men who used them for fun and did not care to marry them.

The pain of not having your own child is devastating to many women in Africa. To them, motherhood is vital for sustaining their marriage and helping avoid troubles from mothers-in-law who are desperate to prove that their sons are men enough to bear them grandchildren.

Many people do not understand that a man too can have medical problems that can cause infertility in marriage. People sometimes forget or do not know that a man could transfer STDs such as gonorrhea and chlamydia to his girlfriend for years before they marry and that the complications of STDs in both sex partners due to partial or late treatment may be the underlying cause of infertility. Yet society invariably blames only the woman.

A master's-level education in epidemiology and international health at the University of Alabama School of Public Health at Birmingham (UAB), Alabama, helped me to further understand how the dynamics of human population changes and socioeconomic burdens can worsen infectious disease epidemics.

I have seen similar complications from STDs and HIV/AIDS and heard histories of how people got STDs and HIV from their sex partners in the U.S., just as it was in Ghana. I heard these stories while I was working as an internal medicine resident physician at the Good

Samaritan Hospital in Baltimore, Maryland, and then at the Medical College of Georgia hospital in Augusta, Georgia.

For the past three years, I have worked at the Duval County Health Department in Jacksonville, Florida, where I am involved in STD/HIV contact investigations. I helped many people from many cultural and ethnic backgrounds get tested and get treatment for STD/HIV. I have learned again that STD/HIV infections know no boundaries. People throughout the world who have STD/HIV-related risky lifestyles can be affected by the negative consequences of STD/HIV infections. The burden can be devastating for poor men and women with other destructive behaviors such as exchanging sex for money, drugs, or other items and having many sex partners.

The memories of those painful experiences working with such unfortunate women has motivated me to spend part of my career to find out what I can do to help more people to increase their STD/HIV knowledge. I want to motivate people to acquire a level of understanding from my practical experiences, which I believe will be helpful to those who are ready to take on the responsibility. I want people to love themselves more and love their sex partners, yet demonstrate that act of love by giving their future sex partners the chance to test for STD/HIV. I want people to protect each other from the complications of STD/HIV—suffering and death.

During this serious HIV epidemic, people can make mistakes about their sexual lifestyle decisions. Such mistakes have sent millions to their graves early. Many more continue to bear the pain of not being able to accomplish their dreams because they are living with HIV/AIDS. The era has come and now is the time that those who love their sexual life and take unnecessary risk that can lead to death will find it. Those who are careful and able to choose a sex partner who will limit sex to each other only will continue to enjoy what sex is meant to be: true unconditional love, responsibility to care and protect each other, and reproduce another human life without STDs and HIV/AIDS. Unsafe sex for fun is a risky choice and a path to early suffering and death.

Therefore, the purpose of this book is to encourage people to increase their knowledge about sexually transmitted diseases including human immunodeficiency virus (HIV) and acquired immunodeficiency syndrome (AIDS), to talk sincerely and openly to a sex partner, and to have an STD/HIV prevention action plan. This book reminds us not to live in denial but to seek urgent treatment and care for STD/HIV, to give a sex partner the chance to benefit from testing and treatment to prevent complications, and to help health care workers to confidentially intervene and prevent the spread of STD/HIV.

The dynamics of STD/HIV infection

The behavioral lifestyle of making risky choices and the socioeconomic burdens that create dependent behavior of sex for money, drugs, and other items as well as the transmission process of STD/HIV to sex partners is what I refer to as the dynamics of STD/HIV infection. It is explained further in chapter two under the subtitle "Modify STD/HIV risk behavior."

STD/HIV infections are diseases that can be acquired by having sex with someone who already has it. STDs can be transferred from one person to another person and can create a significant burden on our health. According to the Centers for Disease Control and Prevention (CDC), an estimated nineteen million new cases of sexually transmitted disease occur in the U.S. each year with a direct medical cost of $13 billion annually.

An estimated 12.9 percent to 19.9 percent of a sample population of homeless people living in a shelter may have STDs—most commonly chlamydia and gonorrhea—without showing any symptoms at all. Community STD screening surveys in some of the major U.S. cities have found that one in four (25 percent) of the people tested in certain areas have STDs.

Anytime someone decides to have sex, there is the chance of getting any of the fourteen sexually transmitted diseases. Nine of these STDs are very common. Three of them—HIV, hepatitis B, and hepatitis C—are deadly and the complications of two of them in the brain--syphilis and herpes---is serious. There is no cure for HIV, and there is no vaccine for prevention, even after more than twenty-five years of vaccine research by many medical scientists. Yet many of us are in denial that we can get HIV by the sexual behavior choices we are making. Many people are not making any effort to modify their sexual behavior until they test positive for HIV. There are other people who know that they are HIV positive and wrongly continue to spread the infection by having unprotected sex.

The complications of STDs can significantly affect a women's ability to get pregnant and can cause infertility. HIV infection and the opportunistic infections associated with end stage HIV, known as acquired immunodeficiency syndrome (AIDS), has significant negative effects on vital organs like the brain, the heart, the kidneys, the eyes, the lungs, and the intestine. Dementia, mental health problems notably depression, kidney failure, recurrent pneumonia, and chronic diarrhea are among the numerous complications that occur with HIV infection.

Therefore, it is very important that every person consider seriously the fact that STD/HIV are diseases that can affect a person's quality of life, productivity, and how long a person will live and suffer from the effects of these diseases before death.

Global burden of STD/HIV infections

The global disease burden of HIV is overwhelming and continues to increase in every part of the world. We must not think of HIV as a disease affecting only the people of Africa and men who have sex with men. The World Health Organization (WHO) estimated that in the U.S., about 1.1 million adults from the age of 15 years and children were living with HIV/AIDS by 2003. There was an expected increase by approximately 100,000 to 1.2 million by 2005. More heterosexual black women, African American men, and young men under 24 years who have sex with other men are getting HIV infection at increasing rates in the U.S.

The WHO AIDS epidemic update estimated that HIV had caused twenty million deaths and thirty-six million people were infected with HIV by December 2001. The update estimated that 39.5 million people in the world were living with HIV by December 2006. There were 4.3 million new infections in 2006 with 2.8 million (approximately 65 percent of the new infections) occurring in Sub-Saharan Africa. HIV/AIDS is the leading cause of death in Africa and the fourth leading cause of death worldwide.

The U.S. government has made enormous financial provisions for its citizens to prevent, treat and control HIV/AIDS. The U.S. congress established Ryan White Care Act in 1990. The Ryan White Program provide funding to cities, states and other public or private non-profit entities to develop, organize, coordinate and operate systems for the delivery of Health Care including AIDS Drug Assistance Program (ADAP) and supportive services. Approximately 2.1 billion US dollars was spent by Ryan White Program for the Federal Fiscal Year (FY) from October1, 2007 through September 30, 2008, FY2008. (Source: The Henry J. Kaiser Family Foundation, statehealthfacts.org).

About 24.7 million people in Sub-Saharan Africa were living with HIV by December 2006 and 2. 9 million died from AIDS-related illnesses. Most people in Africa have no access to HIV medical care and cannot afford a subsidized HIV medication from international organizations. The U.S. President's Emergency Plan for AIDS Relief (PEPFAR) initiated by President G.W. Bush, has provided $15 billion over five years since January 2003 to help fourteen countries in Africa and the Caribbean, which are most affected by HIV/AIDS, to treat approximately 2 million HIV/AIDS patients and prevent 7 million new infections in Botswana, Cote d'Ivoire, Ethiopia, Kenya, Mozambique, Namibia, Nigeria, Rwanda, South Africa, Tanzania, Uganda, Zambia, Guyana, and Haiti. These countries account for approximately fifty percent (50%) of HIV infections Worldwide. PEPFAR has over 1.6 million persons getting HIV medications (also known as HAART) in these countries and is helping to reduce AIDS death rates.

From United States Agency for International Development (USAID) report, the country Cote d'Ivoire in West Africa, has the highest percentage (7.1%) of its citizens living with HIV/AIDS from the ages of 15-49 in West Africa. The HIV/AIDS prevalence of 7.1% has remained stable for the past decade and reports of recent declines among pregnant women in urban areas as of 2005 has been noted by

National AIDS Indicator Survey. As of September 30, 2008, PEPFAR has helped approximately 50,500 HIV positive persons to receive HIV medications and 12,800 HIV positive pregnant women received HIV medication as a prophylactic treatment to prevent the vertical transmission of HIV from mother to new born babies (other source: UNAIDS, Report on Global AIDS Epidemic, 2008).

Nigeria is located in West Africa. It is one of the countries in Sub-Saharan Africa. Reports from USAID estimates a population of approximately 140 million as at 2005 and 3.1% of adults from ages 15-49 have HIV/AIDS (in other words, HIV/AIDS prevalence rate of 3.1%). An estimated total of 2.5 million of people of ages 0-49 are living with HIV in Nigeria by the end of 2007 (other source: UNAIDS, Report on Global AIDS Epidemic 2008). The country has been significantly affected by HIV/AIDS and now accounts for nearly ten percent (10%) of the HIV/AIDS burden in the World with estimated four million of its citizens HIV positive from a report in march, 2009 (source-http://www.usaid.gov/ng/so14.htm). PEPFAR by working with the government in Nigeria, has helped 211,500 HIV positive individual to receive medication for HIV/AIDS and approximately 27,000 HIV positive pregnant women have received HIV prophylactic treatment to prevent the transmission of HIV from mother to the new born babies. Political will by the government of Nigeria to work with community to reduce HIV/AIDS is important. Nigeria is a rich nation and can learn from the leadership of United States President and then use the country's vast natural, human and financial resources and public health expertise to team up with the community and control HIV/AIDS.

Similar global efforts by PEPFAR to help Africa is noted in South Africa. The USAID reports that country has a population of 47.9 million (an estimated population at the end of 2007) and continue to benefit from PEPFAR's HIV prevention and control plan. South Africa is one of the countries with the highest number of HIV/AIDS. Approximately 18.1% of adults from ages 19-49 are living with HIV/AIDS. Children and adults of ages 0-49 living with HIV/AIDS at the end of 2007 were about 5.7 million and then 549, 700 of them received HIV medications. HIV prophylactic treatment has been given to about 333,100 HIV positive pregnant women by PEPFAR to protect new born babies from HIV infection in South Africa.

In the Carribean, the country Haiti is noted to have HIV prevalence rate of 2.2% for adults of ages 15-49. An estimated 120,000 of Haitians from ages 0-49 were living with HIV at the end of 2007. The USAID reports that PEPFAR has helped 17,700 HIV positive persons to receive HIV medications at September 30, 2008 and about 3, 200 pregnant HIV positive women were treated with HIV medication to prevent their babies from getting HIV infection (other source: UNAIDS, Report on Global AIDS Epidemic, 2008).

In the Latin America, Mexico has done well to keep HIV/AIDS under control by the end of 2005. Although most people in Mexico maintain heterosexual relationship between a man and a woman like the Africa countries but, unlike most Africa Countries, Mexico has low HIV prevalence rate of less than 1% and an estimated 180,000 of the 103 million Mexicans were living with HIV/AIDS at the end of 2005. Mexico's HIV prevalence of less than 1% is mostly restricted to the men who have sex with men (MSM) and commercial sex workers.

Latin America and the Caribbean had an estimated 1.4 million adults and children infected with HIV/AIDS by December 2000 compared to 1.3 million in December 1999. All of these statistics indicate that HIV infection continues to increase all over the world, and we need to actively prevent and control it.

It is very important to know that estimated rates of HIV have increased more than 50 percent in some areas of Eastern Europe and Central Asia since 2004. An estimated 8.6 million cases were reported in Asia. In India, 2.5 million people were living with HIV infection in December 2006. In China, HIV infection was as high as 82 percent among injection drug users and 6 percent in commercial sex workers during 1998–1999. By January 1999, approximately 10,000 HIV cases were reported in the Russian Federation, and by December 2000, a cumulative increase to 70,000 was reported.

We must actively encourage people to test and detect HIV infection early and then enroll HIV positive patients in programs to ensure optimum care and lifestyle modifications that will reduce the spread of HIV infection.

The cost of HIV treatment is expensive, but governments throughout the world have made plans to subsidize the treatment. Estimates in 2002 show that each HIV infection costs between $50,000 to $100,000 per year (in U.S. dollars) to treat in Western Europe and North America when the full set of drug combinations and other medical practices are used. In 2002, Brazil had the lowest prices for HIV treatment with drugs, but the drugs alone without adding the cost of medical care and hospital treatment was $2,700 per year (World Health Organization 2003).

Current reductions in the prices of medication used for treating HIV and improvement in the cost-effectiveness of combining medications into fewer pills a day is a positive action taken by medical personnel who think about the poor and people suffering from a disease that has no cure for now. However, noncompliance with treatment by HIV patients is commonly associated with the development of drug resistance. This means that the drug loses the potency to kill HIV and may further increase the cost of treatment. For instance, a newly approved medication, raltegravir, for treating resistant HIV cases, costs $27 a day, so $10,000 a year must be added to the usual multiple drug combination regimen to treat a resistant case of HIV.

The cost of care is too expensive for HIV patients in developing countries especially in Africa. Donor countries, organizations, and PEPFAR may have to spend more money to help with treatment and prevention of HIV infection in both developed and developing countries if more effort is not made to help individuals modify their sex behaviors and have an STD/HIV prevention action plan. A lot of people do not realize that although they can make decisions to have whatever kind of sex life they want, when they get sick, their medical care affects them physically and mentally, and also affects their families and the government budget. STD/HIV infection becomes a problem for the entire community because it is an infection that can be passed on to other people with the added financial burden and suffering.

Imagine how much financial burden a young man or woman at the age of 20 might have and the financial and socioeconomic burden on the government if a young person has HIV infection that has no cure. The financial and socioeconomic burden on individuals, families, and the government will worsen if those who have HIV infection and know that they are HIV positive negligently continue to expose other people to it without giving the sex partners the chance to make an informed decision to protect themselves.

The STD/HIV prevention action must involve individual action plans, family, government, community-based organizations (CBOs), community leaders, non-governmental organizations (NGOs), worldwide organizations like WHO, World Bank, United States Agency for International Development (USAID), and health care facilities such as hospitals, clinics, and public health services.

This book provides important information about individual STD/HIV prevention action plans for those who do not have HIV infection and lifestyle modification for those who are living with STD/HIV infection. I hope this information may help all of us to slow the spread of HIV infection until a cure or vaccine for HIV is found.

The knowledge acquired by reading this book should encourage individuals especially the youth to understand the following core messages:

- Prevent undue suffering when making choices about their sex life.

- Test together with your sex partner for STD/HIV and verify each others' results before sex. This is as an act of responsibility and love.

- Practice abstinence.

- Limit sex to one person who will limit sex to you in marriage (monogamy).

- Notify sex partners of STD/HIV positive results.

- Use protection such as condoms.

- Modify dependent sexual behavior to avoid STD/HIV and early suffering and death from HIV, hepatitis B and hepatitis C and the complications of syphilis and herpes as well as the complications of chlamydia and gonorrhea such as PID and infertility.

- Note the role of policymakers to help communities to control the HIV epidemic.

1

The effects of sexually transmitted diseases on the human reproductive system

The knowledge of female and male reproductive organs is very important to help us to understand how STDs can affect our life and fertility.

The female and the male reproductive organs are uniquely designed parts of the human body. Together with the biological chemicals called hormones secreted by endocrine glands that control their functions, the reproductive organs have been intelligently designed to make sure the reproduction of a baby, another human being, is achieved. STDs can change this unique ability of a man and a woman to reproduce another human being. [Hormones are defined as biological chemicals secreted by specialized glands in the body called endocrine glands. Examples of endocrine glands involved in reproduction are the pituitary glands, adrenal gland, and the ovaries.]

Anatomy of female reproductive organs

The female reproductive system is made up of the vagina, cervix, uterus (womb), left and right fallopian tubes (tubes), left and right ovaries, and supporting structures called ligaments. See figure 1a. Each one of these organs has special functions in a female. The vagina is a muscular tube lined with epithelial cells. [Epithelial cells are layers of cells, which usually cover the surfaces of tissues and organs of the body.]

The vagina is specially designed for the penis, sex, and the birth of a baby. It can expand and has a unique way of protecting itself from infection by secreting lubricating acidic fluid (pH of 3.5–4.5) that prevents infection. However, STDs can change this unique method of preservation and expose a woman to complications of STD/HIV.

Figure 1a. Female reproductive system

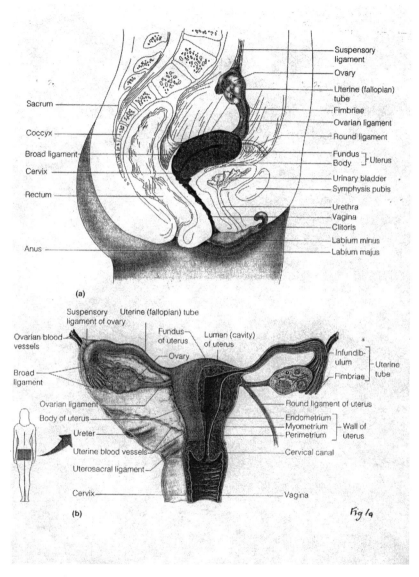

The womb (uterus) is a muscular tube with epithelial lining that is suspended into the vagina by ligaments and muscles. The lower part of the womb that projects into the vagina is called the cervix. The top part of the womb extends into the belly (abdomen). Attached to the sides of the top part of the womb are the left and the right tubes (fallopian tubes). The free ends of the tubes called fimbriae are very mobile and extend close to the front part of the left and right ovaries. The space in the vagina continues through the cervix and the womb to the ends of the tubes.

It is amazing how this reproductive system has been intelligently designed for the main purposes of sexual activity that can result in the conception and reproduction of a baby, another human being. The ovaries produce eggs (oocytes), which contain genetic material called deoxyribonucleic acid (DNA) by the middle day of every month of the menstrual cycle. The DNA of the egg meets with the DNA inside the sperm to produce a baby. The ovaries are uniquely protected from STDs by not being directly attached to the tubes. Otherwise, infections from STDs can spread easily to the ovaries and destroy the DNA and the ability of a woman to have a baby.

The fimbriae are set into motion like a fan in front of the ovary to direct the egg, which contains the DNA released from the ovary, by the middle day of the calendar of the menses (menstrual cycle) so that the egg will enter the tube where it will meet with the sperm and get fertilized to form one structure called the zygote. The zygote moves down the tube into the womb and attaches to the womb. The cells continue to divide and go through multiple of divisions and multiplications, differentiation and development many times as the zygote forms a baby.

Effects of STD and abortions

STDs in women can cause these complications:

- Salpingitis (inflammation of the tubes)

- Pelvic inflammatory disease (PID) (inflammation of the fallopian tubes and the nearby structures of the female reproductive system in the pelvis, which can lead to a pool of infected fluid in the pelvis, called a pelvic abscess)

- Tubal stricture (narrowing of the space in the fallopian tubes)

- Ectopic pregnancy (pregnancy and development of a baby outside the womb)

- Pelvic abscess

- Infertility (the inability of a woman to get pregnant naturally and give birth after twelve months of unprotected sexual intercourse)

Whenever a woman is having sex, she should know her ability to get pregnant and give birth, as described here, could be changed if she gets STDs such as chlamydia or gonorrhea and is not treated completely for a cure. A delay of treatment and also numerous repeated infections of STDs can cause inflammation of the tubes and the nearby structures (causing pelvic inflammatory disease), scarring, narrowing (stricture), and blockage of the tubes so that the zygote cannot move down the tubes into the uterus to grow and form the baby. In such cases, the zygote starts the entire development of the baby in the tube that is outside the womb (causing an ectopic pregnancy). As the baby grows, the tube will burst (ruptured ectopic pregnancy). This complication can cause the death of the woman if it is not diagnosed early because there will be continuous bleeding and loss of blood. A lot of young women die from ruptured ectopic pregnancies all over the world, and especially in Africa and other developing countries where there is delay in seeking medical care.

When the ruptured tube is repaired by surgery or removed because it cannot be repaired, the function of the tubes to transport the egg and the sperm is impaired. Then the woman becomes infertile and cannot naturally get pregnant. In some cases the sperm and the egg cannot meet at all because the tubes are completely blocked.

In other cases, the inflammation due to the STDs may be very severe and spread into the ovaries. A pool of infected fluid (pus) will form in the tubes, ovaries, and space around them (creating a tubo-ovarian abscess). The entire structure will need to be removed to prevent the infection from spreading to the rest of the body and prevent death. The woman's ability to bear a child naturally is then lost if both tubes are affected by inflammation from STDs. She is said to be infertile.

In case a pregnancy occurs and a woman decides to have an abortion, it should be remembered that the scraping of the lining of the uterus by dilation and curettage (D&C) can result in the loss of the lining of the uterus, scarring, and near closure of the space inside the uterus (uterus synaeche) that will later make it difficult for the attachment (implantation) of the product of fertilization (zygote) to the uterus and the formation of a baby. This is also a cause of infertility.

When abortion is not done properly and the antibiotic treatment is not good enough, a serious infection called septic abortion may develop. Septic abortion means the woman's reproductive system is infected after an abortion. This condition is deadly if not treated early. Septic abortion is more common in Africa and developing countries especially when people who pose as doctors (quack doctors) perform abortion and give all kinds of herbs or drugs to a pregnant woman. A quack doctor is not professionally trained or certified as a doctor. Treatment from a quack doctor can be a life-threatening complication of abortion—a needless and harmful consequence of sexual behavior—and put the lives of many women at risk of death.

There have been many cases in the developing countries, especially in Africa, where young women who had such septic abortion procedures by quack doctors came to the hospitals with perforation of the uterus. These women had to undergo complete surgical removal of the uterus in the hospital and about two weeks of antibiotic treatment. With no reproductive organs, they lose the ability to get pregnant for the rest of their lives.

Every woman should remember that if she wants to have children, STDs might prevent that from happening. Therefore, a woman should be careful to make sure that a man does not pass any STDs to her. The only way to be sure is to test and make sure the man also tests for STDs. Both results need to be verified, and both sexual partners need to discuss STD/HIV prevention and protection before committing to a sexual relationship.

This process of testing to make sure that a woman will not start having sex with a man who already has STD/HIV is very important and one of the best things a woman who wants to bear children can do for herself and her family. A complete treatment and cure for STDs in both the woman and the man is also important to preserve the fertility of a woman. Anyone who wants to have children should not think of sex as intended only for fun. Think of it for both fertility and as an intimate relationship to preserve the dignity of a woman.

Anatomy of male reproductive organs

The male reproductive system consists of the penis, ejaculatory duct, epididymis, testes, and the secretory glands (in other words, these are bulbourethral glands, prostate gland, and seminal vesicles which secrete fluids that transport sperm).

Figure 1b. Male reproductive system

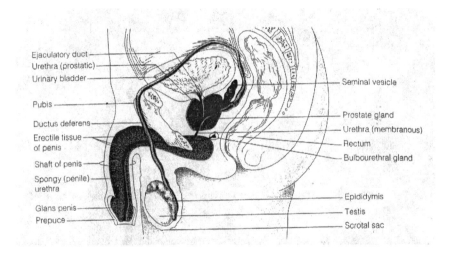

The testes produce the sperm. The sperm is stored in the epididymis. Before the sperm is released, the bulbourethral gland secretes a clear and sticky fluid to flush out the traces of urine in the urethra of the penis to make sure that no urine contaminates the sperm, which contain vital DNA for the formation of a baby. The sticky fluid also lubricates the vagina.

The secretion of the prostate gland and the seminal vesicles is called semen. Semen contains vitamin C and a certain kind of sugar called fructose to nourish the sperm, seminal plasmin that prevents bacterial infection, prostaglandin, and the hormone relaxin that helps the sperm to move through the vagina, cervix, uterus, and the tubes to meet the egg and fertilize it. The sperm must be produced in an adequate amount (more than 20 million/ml) and carried in a unique medium (semen) of pH 7.4 similar to the pH of blood to preserve it as a living cell. Sperm must be healthy enough to move through the ejaculatory duct and then in the semen through the urethra of the penis into the vagina to enter the uterus and the fallopian tube. Overall, the sperm must be more than 40 percent mobile for fertilization of the oocyte (egg) of the female to occur.

Effects of STD complications in males

STDs can cause complications in the male reproductive system. When STDs such as gonorrhea and chlamydia are not completely treated and cured, it causes inflammation of the urethra of the penis, scarring, and narrowing (stricture) as the man advances in age. This complication will make it difficult for the man to pass urine later in life, urine retention, and, if not treated early, infection and retained urine will back up into the kidneys and cause kidney failure. When the kidney failure is not diagnosed early and treated, it is usually deadly especially in Africa and the developing countries where there is no continuous dialysis care.

The spread of STD inflammation to the epididymis (epididymitis) and the testes (orchitis) or both the epididymis and the testes (epididymoorchitis) may case scarring and reduction in the number of healthy sperm produced and, in some cases, loss of the ability of the man's sperm to fertilize the egg. The man may not be able to naturally conceive a baby with a woman and may be the cause of infertility in marriage.

STDs can affect a man's chances of being a natural father of a baby in addition to the risk of getting dangerous infectious diseases like HIV, hepatitis B, hepatitis C and syphilis. A man is always encouraged to test for STD together with the female sex partner, verify results, and ensure complete treatment to help preserve his fertility, the health and the fertility of a female sex partner.

2

STD patient and sex partner behavior modifications

It is unfortunate that many people are in denial of the fact that they can get sexually transmitted diseases and HIV infection from having casual sex at clubs and parties, having sex without condoms, having multiple sexual partners, sharing needles to inject drugs, or trading sex for drugs and money.

Individual STD prevention action plans must be a very important part of every person's life even though the HIV epidemic is not taken seriously by many people until they get HIV infection.

STD/HIV knowledge gap and lack of sustained prevention action

The youth and young adults age 15–24 seem to have an STD/HIV prevention knowledge gap. They adopt lifestyles like many people who had similar lifestyles and have either died from HIV infection and complications of AIDS or are now living with HIV/AIDS. Perhaps the young adults, who were too young to understand or were not born at the peak of the HIV/AIDS epidemic health education and at the peak of increased death due to AIDS in 1993 and prior to the use of highly active antiretroviral therapy (HAART) for HIV, have underestimated the burden of HIV infection and complications of AIDS.

These young people must be reminded that the chances of getting HIV infection are higher than in the past years because many people who have HIV infection are living a little longer with difficult life-changing diseases and complications. Most HIV positive patients are still sexually active. Most importantly, people who have a new HIV infection may not be aware of their HIV status. Although such people may look handsome or beautiful and attractive, they have proved to be highly infectious and more likely to spread the infection to many other sex partners before they are diagnosed as having HIV/AIDS.

Many people are not testing together or at the same time with their sex partners before sex. People must be encouraged to test and verify to make sure that the sex partner has no STD/HIV infection before beginning a sexual relationship. Although many people have a plan to use condoms and will mention that they will use condom protection, they forget to use them all the time with all sex partners. As a consequence, they become exposed to HIV infection especially at a time of their lives when drinking alcohol and beer and using drugs such as crack cocaine, marijuana, heroin, methamphetamine, and many other mood changing drugs which affects their judgment and causes them to take risks by having sex with someone who has STD/HIV.

Any time a person starts having sex with the wrong person without testing for STD/HIV, that person puts his or her life and safety on the line for a reduced quality of life after HIV infection, which has no cure. Many people are meeting the wrong sex partners on Web sites over the Internet. They use fake names and do not care about the sex partner except to have sex. Such anonymous and wrong sex partners will refuse to get tested for STD/HIV and or verify results before sex. They will keep their HIV status and where they live and their sexual lifestyle secret from the sex partner. They may have many other sex partners, never commit to only one sex partner and usually infect men who have sex with men (MSM) and women with STD/HIV. It is not worth the money or the attraction of the person's looks. None of those is worth more than anyone's life. Therefore, everybody must be careful, have an STD/HIV prevention action plan, and stay alive.

Many young people are choosing to entrust their bodies to the wrong sex partners and start having sex with people whose full name and lifestyle they don't know. People who risk getting involved in such sexual relationships are encouraged to remember that when it is later found out that the person has passed on STD/HIV, all the trust in the relationship disappears. Sexual love may turn to hatred, regrets, and depression for not making the right decision to protect yourselves.

People are perishing from HIV because of lack of knowledge. In many instances, there is the lack of knowledge that the sex partners have STD/HIV, the HIV diseases process and complications, and have no prevention action plan or fail to consistently do an STD/HIV prevention action plan. Reading and applying the STD/HIV prevention knowledge to stay safe with someone who actually cares about the sex partner is important. Believe it or not, a person's sex life will affect how long that person lives on earth during this period of the HIV epidemic.

Let us remember that those who have previously had STDs have a higher chance of getting the infection again. For women, repeated (recurrent) infections with chlamydia and gonorrhea can cause PID, scarring and blockage of the tubes, ectopic pregnancy and infertility. For both men and women, it is a sign of impending HIV infection. In fact, many people who have HIV infection have had STDs in the past months to years before HIV diagnosis. History of STDs is a warning sign that a consistent HIV prevention plan is necessary now.

Chlamydia, gonorrhea, and many other STDs will cause a sore (inflammation) that makes it easier for HIV to enter a person's blood and spread to other parts of the body. Therefore, the presence of other STDs increases the chance of getting HIV when a person has sex with an HIV positive sex partner.

Sex in the mouth (oral sex) or the anus and rectum (anal sex) can expose people to STD/HIV infection. The mouth is likely to have sores and bleeding spots in the gums that may not be obvious but will be sites for transmission of STD/HIV. The anus and rectum are not anatomically structured to withstand the pressure of sexual activity. Therefore, there is likely to be bruising, bleeding, and sores by having anal sex ("sex in the butt") and the risk of transmission of STD/HIV. It cannot be predicted what will happen when the DNA of the sperm is deposited in a culture medium of stool with all kinds of bacteria and viruses in the anus and rectum of a person. Remember that some of the virus and bacteria can change or multiply when they get into contact with human DNA and proteins.

Many adolescents think that having oral sex will not give them a sexually transmitted disease, but that is a mistake. STD/HIV can be transmitted by oral sex, and indeed STDs such as syphilis, gonorrhea, chlamydia, HPV, and herpes have been diagnosed from sores and swabs of the mouth and throat of both men and women.

The high prevalence of HIV in men who have sex with men and the fact that the anus and the rectum are more likely to bruise and bleed and develop sores from the pressure of anal sexual intercourse increases the chance that anal sex will likely expose a person to HIV infection and other STDs. This fact is obvious from HIV data for the past twenty-five years. Since HIV was first diagnosed in 1981 and for more than twenty-five years since the epidemic of HIV/AIDS, approximately 75 percent of all HIV cases have been diagnosed in men in countries such as the U.S. where men who have sex with men continue to have high numbers of new and old cases of HIV diagnoses. Young adolescent males should assess their chances of living with HIV when making informed decisions about choosing sex partners. When men choose to have sex with men then these are the negative consequences that are found to be common in MSM than any other sexual lifestyle.

1. HIV/AIDS and its complications. In case of an African American man, the chance of getting HIV infection is about 50% (this means you can get HIV infection about one out of every two African American MSM sex partners you choose) since 46% of African American men who are MSM have HIV infection (Source: CDC, HIV/AIDS and Men Who Have Sex With Men). More MSM have HIV infection than any other sex defined group in the U.S.

2. STDs cause sores of rectum (proctitis) and especially syphilis and Hepatitis C is more common in HIV positive

15

MSM and those who abuse injection of drugs than any other group.

3. Incontenence of stool especially those who practice fisting (hand in rectum).

4. Tear (fissure) in anus and its complications such as infection with fluid (pus) collection (known as anal abscess), a tract of connection of rectum to skin of anus (fistula-in-anus).

5. Cancer of anus, usually as a complication of genital warts caused by human papilloma virus (HPV) especially when the infected person has HIV/AIDS.

6. Karposi's sarcoma, a cancer most commonly found in MSM who have HIV/AIDS.

Global STD/HIV risk behavior and the spread of STD/HIV

These are the risky behaviors (risk factors) that increase a person's chances of getting STDs and HIV/AIDS infections:

- Having sex with a new sex partner without both of you testing for STD/HIV

- Multiple sex partners

- Inconsistent use of condoms

- A sex partner younger than 25

- Commercial sex partners (male and female prostitutes)

- Men who have sex with men

- Drug abuse

Drug abuse (the intravenous drug use [IDU] and the use of drugs like alcohol, methamphetamine, cocaine, and marijuana) especially at clubs and parties increases the risk of people making mistakes and having sex with someone they do not know or would not have chosen for sex. There are many anecdotal reports of people getting STDs and HIV infection in this manner of drug use and sexual activity. [IDU describes the injection of mood changing drugs such as heroin. Drug users get intoxicated with such drugs and the IV drug users mistakenly share needles and syringes, from which they get infections such as HIV, hepatitis B and C.]

HIV can spread quickly among intravenous drug users (IDUs). The spread of HIV has been noted among IDUs in New York City in the 1980s, and in Edinburgh (the United Kingdom), Bangkok (Thailand), Ho Chi Minh City (Vietnam), Santos (Brazil), Odessa (Ukraine), Svetlogorsk (Belarus), and Moscow and Irkutsak (the Russian Federation). In 2001, the CDC noted the similar spread of HIV among those who inject drugs in Narva (Estonia), in an entire province in India, in Yunnan in China and across countries such as Myanmar.

In some areas, the cases of HIV among those who inject drugs increased from less than 5 percent to over 40 percent in a period of twelve months. At Manipur in India, the number of existing cases of HIV increased from less than 10 percent to more than 60 percent in six months. In Eastern Europe, where HIV was found to be increasing after 1996, 80–90 percent of new HIV infections were found among IV drug users in 2001, and the epidemic of HIV was the fastest growing in the world (World Health Organization 2003).

Injection of drugs such as heroin can play a critical role in the spread of HIV to broader populations through sexual relationships between a man and a woman (heterosexual transmission) or men having sex with men (homosexual transmission) and through a mother to child (vertical transmission). For example, in Manipur, 45 percent of the regular sexual partners of HIV positive IDUs acquired the virus over a six-year period (World Health Organization 2003). From 1996–2001, most of the HIV positive infants in Ukraine and the Russian Federation were born to mothers who were IDUs or sex partners of IDUs (World Health Organization 2003). It has been observed that many female IDUs get involved in selling sex to support their own or a male sex partner's drug use practices while many prostitutes get introduced to drug use by their male drug-user partners.

The study among IDUs in Dhaka (Bangladesh) in 1997 found that 10 percent of male IDUs had experienced male to male sex. The efficiency of transmission of HIV through unprotected heterosexual relationships by vaginal intercourse can be as much as ten times higher from a man to a woman than from a woman to a man.

Most cases of chlamydia and gonorrhea are diagnosed in females throughout the world but HIV is commonly diagnosed in men except in Africa and other developing countries. Sexual transmission of HIV continues to be the main mode of spread of HIV infection. Therefore, in countries where more men have sex with men, such as in the U.S., more cases of HIV are diagnosed in men; whereas, in countries in Africa and other developing nations where most men can have far more female sex partners and there is a low rate of condom usage, more HIV infections are diagnosed in women. Thus, males continue to be the most determinant host and factor for the spread of STD/HIV infections since they invariably get to take charge of the act of deciding what kind of sexual intercourse should occur and whether to use a condom or not when they are ready to have sex. Women are therefore encouraged to negotiate for abstinence until marriage, and if they decide to have sex before marriage, they must negotiate for testing to verify HIV results and condom use always for their own safety and that of their children. Remember ATBC: Abstinence, Test and verify HIV results before sex, Be faithful to commit to one sex partner in marriage (monogamy) and Condom use always may help to prevent STD/HIV.

Modify STD/HIV risk behavior

It is important to understand the dynamics of the transmission and spread of STD/HIV so that you can modify your sex life to prevent coming into contact with STD/HIV infections. Men have more HIV infections than women, so the fact that men need to protect women from HIV infection in a monogamous sexual relationship is vital to the control of HIV. The proper and consistent use of condoms by men and women who decide to have more than one sex partner is similarly vital to limit the spread of STD/HIV infection. Female IDUs and female partners of male IDUs have increased risk of getting HIV than male IDUs. For example, in the Russian Federation, it is estimated that 90 percent of the estimated 1 million HIV infections in 2002 were among IDUs. In India and Thailand, studies in 2000–2002 found that the number of people with HIV was increasing partly because there were few interventions to prevent HIV transmission among intravenous drug users (World Health Organization 2003). Avoidance of IDUs, especially for women, is essential to avoid getting HIV infection.

It must be pointed out that for STDs such as HIV, hepatitis B and C, chlamydia and gonorrhea, genital warts and genital herpes, a person can get it anytime there is sexual contact with an infected person;

whereas, a person can get STDs such as syphilis when the sex partner who is the source of syphilis has a primary lesion or a sore or secondary mucous lesion such as condylomata lata. Thus people with early latent and those who have late latent syphilis as less likely to transmit syphilis by sexual contact.

Those who inject drugs are more likely to get hepatitis B or hepatitis C infection in addition to HIV and spread these infections to their sex partners as noted from persons J to M in diagram I on page 23 and persons E to W in diagram II on page 25. Therefore, individuals who inject themselves with drugs should not share needles and syringes. They must be encouraged to use condoms and prevent the spread of HIV, hepatitis B, and hepatitis C infection to their sex partners like persons M and K in diagram I. It is also recommended that such people should abstain from sex at the time of using drugs to avoid making the mistake of having sex with someone they do not know as was done by persons E and T in diagram II and to avoid the mistake of having group sex at parties and sex clubs like persons T, P, and V in diagram II because such risky behaviors will most likely expose them and their sex partners to STD/HIV infections.

It is a known fact that men who have sex with men (MSM) like persons B, R, and L in diagram I have a higher chance of getting HIV infection. More men have HIV infection than women by a ratio of approximately 3:1 since the onset of the HIV epidemic in 1981 in the U.S. Therefore, it is more likely for men who have sex with men to get HIV infection. A process of making young men aware of this fact about MSM is very important to enable them to make informed decisions and think seriously before making such a decision to become MSM and getting HIV infection. Living with HIV infection for the rest of your life and the complications of AIDS is no joke. The danger of getting HIV infection is real for MSM.

Anonymous sex partners like R in diagram I are killing many people with STD/HIV, yet a lot of people like B in diagram I are making mistakes by risking everything including their life and body to have sex with R, someone they don't even know. Depending on a person like R and B to exchange sex for money is like selling your life in the era of HIV/AIDS infections. Dependent behaviors are driving many people such as persons R and H in diagram I and persons W and T in diagram II and especially women and MSM to their graves. Carefully consider these real life situations and avoid getting HIV infection.

At this time we do not have a cure for HIV infection. People could avoid "old sex partner syndrome" and "new sex partner syndrome" as illustrated by diagram I and diagram II, respectively. Old sex partner syndrome is a situation in which a person A with no history of STD/HIV starts getting symptoms and signs of STD/HIV after renewing the act of having sex again with old sex partner B (as shown in diagram I), who unknowingly has changed his behavior and has gotten STD and or HIV from other sex partner(s).

New sex partner syndrome is a situation in which a person G with no history of STD/HIV starts getting symptoms and signs of STD/HIV after having sex with a new sex partner C (as shown in diagram II), who unknowingly has STD and or HIV and other sex partner(s)

In some situations, the sex partners B in diagram I and C in diagram II may know of the already diagnosed STD and or HIV and will not tell sex partner A and G, but in most cases, the sex partners B and C do not know that he or she has already gotten an STD or HIV because of previous or ongoing sexual relationship(s) with other sex partners such as J, L, H, or R in diagram I and Q, F, E, and Z in diagram II, respectively, who have high STD/HIV risk behavior and STD/HIV infections.

Many people can be identified as A. They have symptoms and signs and a diagnosis of STD and or HIV because of old sex partner syndrome when they renewed an old sexual relationship—in some cases with their baby's dad like person B or baby's mother. Many other people have an STD or HIV because of new sex partner syndrome when they made a mistake to start a new sexual relationship without testing and identifying each others' results to make sure there is no STD/HIV.

The young female W in diagram II is dependent on E for sex in exchange for money, so she has a higher chance of getting HIV sometime in the future if no STD/HIV test is done at the beginning of the relationship and both results verified to make sure there is no STD/HIV infection before committing to a sexual relationship. No HIV test was done before sex with E, and female W got an HIV infection. Do not make mistakes like female A and W and person G. Patiently spend time to know your sex partner very well, seek more responsibility to protect each other, and make testing for STD/HIV before sex an act of love.

Diagram I. The dynamics of STD/HIV infection

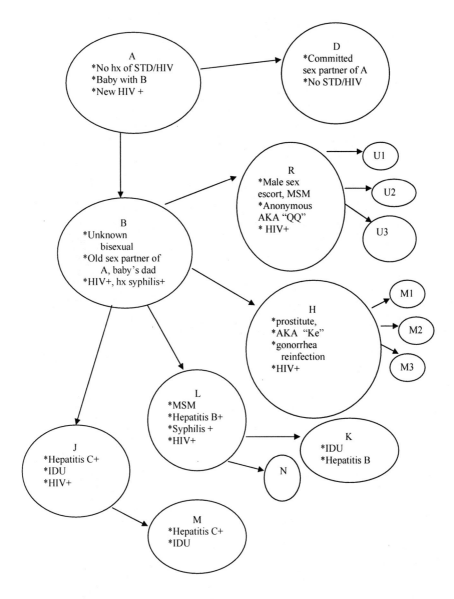

Diagram I. The illustrations are hypothetical but simulate real facts of infection, transmission, and spread of STD/HIV: Individuals who behave as shown in the diagram have higher chance of getting STD/HIV as noted.

U1, U2, and U3 are regular uncommitted sex partners of R, names unknown. R has had 70 sex partners within one year.

M1, M2, and M3 were male sex partners of H at a beach resort and two other clubs, all of them are anonymous sex partners. H has had 240 sex partners within the past year. N is a "one night stand" sex partner of L at a club. They have known each other for two days but shared no details including names. B has a history (hx) of syphilis and had sex with L when there was a sore of primary syphilis, so he spread it to L who was interviewed confidentially and was treated with penicillin G injection for a cure. Sex partner K got the chance to test for syphilis and received prophylactic treatment. B had sex with R, H, and J within twelve months after the healing of primary stage of syphilis. R, H, and J did not test positive for syphilis but need prophylactic treatment of syphilis with penicillin G injection.

Diagram II. The dynamics of STD/HIV infection

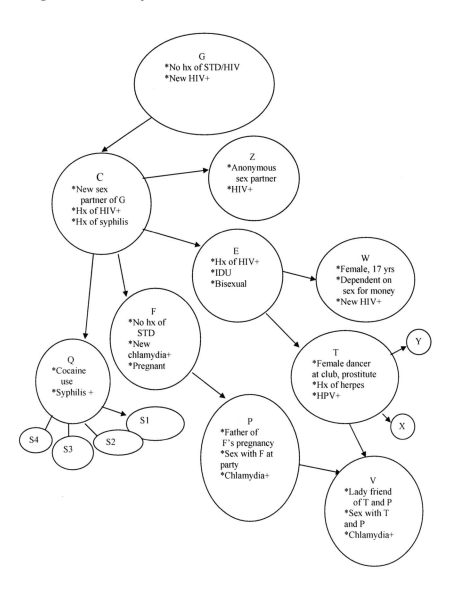

Diagram II. The illustrations are hypothetical but simulate real facts of infection, transmission, and spread of STD/HIV: Q exchanged cocaine for sex with prostitutes S1, S2, S3, and S4, but their names are unknown (they were anonymous sex partners). T has a history (hx) of herpes, which may be a sign of undiagnosed HIV infection spread from E. HPV infection increases her chance of getting cervical cancer especially when she is later diagnosed with HIV/AIDS. In case T had received the HPV vaccine called Gardasil prior to exposure to HPV, it could protect her from getting HPV infection and cervical cancer. F may have come into contact with HIV by having sex with C and has a high risk of transmission of HIV to her baby.

[Note: Consult your doctor about the side effects of Gardasil before your vaccination]

It is a common finding in old and new sex partner syndrome that partner B or C may be bisexual and hides his identity "down low." He may not want to commit to anyone, tell lies about his sex life, have multiple sex partners, or use fake names or addresses. Some people, who can be identified as B, move from state to state and even from country to country just to party and have sex. Sexual relationships with people who have such a lifestyle is a very high STD/HIV risk, so make sure you take time to find out who you are having sex with and know the person very well. Otherwise when the diseases start showing up, you will be left alone to deal with the troubles that are packaged into the consequences of turning a flashy joy into lifelong misery.

To avoid getting STD/HIV from old sex partner syndrome, new sex partner syndrome, uncommitted and lying sex partners in this era where there is no cure for HIV infection, it is advisable to test for STD/HIV and identify a sex partner's recent negative STD/HIV test results.

In cities and places where prostitution has been commercialized, a regulated body of law enforcement officers must consistently verify three- to six-month STD/HIV test results to protect the general public from those who will be soliciting sex for money like R and H in diagram I, because such people can continue to spread a disease like HIV even when they know that they have HIV infection. Such behaviors can worsen the financial burden on the local and federal government budgets to spend more money to treat HIV infections and its opportunistic complications and other STDs.

The government has a duty to care for its citizens. HIV positive patients need support from the government, the community, families, and friends, and at the same time we must put in place sexual behavior modification measures that will enable people to live a healthy and productive life without having too many cases of STD/HIV infections.

In the setting of our so called "private sex life" we must remember that when we contract infectious STD/HIV, our privacy becomes a financial and economic burden for the government and the community like the situation of E and V in diagram II who had no money to pay for their treatment after group sex with W, T and T, P respectively. Therefore, we must endeavor to protect each other from getting STD/HIV infection for whatever sexual lifestyle we choose to adopt.

Unless a modification of sexual lifestyle takes place, a previous or a new history of STD is a clue to impending HIV infection. A previous history of syphilis by person B or a new STD like gonorrhea or chlamydia by a person like H or F implies that a person is involved in a sexual relationship with someone who is within a human chain of multiple transfers of STD/HIV as shown in diagrams I and II. This situation may have one or many HIV patients within the chain of sex partners and will increase the chance of getting HIV someday in the future as it occurs in person H. This finding is usually quite obvious from the analysis of the spread of various stages of syphilis and HIV infections among groups (clusters) of sex partners. In case you have an STD in the past, be careful and take action to modify your sex life immediately because it is a sign of impending HIV spread from a chain of STD/HIV as shown in diagrams I and II.

In our effort to modify our sexual lifestyle, let us encourage each other to be honest about our sex life and look for an honest sex partner who will limit sex to one person. When people are involved in an honest monogamous relationship, a talk and discussion of problems that creates a prolonged anger and periods of no sex with a committed sex partner like D in diagram I should be pursued early to resolve the problems. Previously committed sex partners, like persons A and D in diagram I, should try to forgive each other and forget the past minor issues in order not to allow such issues to override the sex life in a monogamous relationship. Many people such as A and D have allowed anger and unforgiveness of minor issues to get in the way of a committed sex life. By making such a mistake, they have allowed the other previously committed sex partner like A in diagram I, who was not able to wait for a prolonged period of weeks to months without sex, to drift away for sex and get an STD/HIV infection from someone and most probably from an old sex partner like B in diagram I who really does not care about A and does not want to commit to anyone. This is usually the core of the problem that leads to the example of what I refer to as old sex partner syndrome.

Transfers of STD/HIV into many previously committed monogamous sexual relationships have occurred because of petty issues. Stay safe, protect yourself, modify a sexual lifestyle, and have two recent STD/HIV test results within three to six months ready to prove to your new or old sex partner that you can be trusted. Always use condoms if you decide to have sex with someone who is not married to you. Try as much as possible not to behave like sex partners A, B, R, H, L, J, and K in diagram I and G, E, Q, and W in diagram II who made risky choices for sex and behaviors that got them involved in a chain of transmission of deadly hepatitis B, C, and HIV and may expose a baby to HIV infection like persons C, F, and P.

Avoid making mistakes by combining the use of street drugs like cocaine and marijuana with sex like person Q who acquired syphilis and transmitted it to many sex partners like S1–S4 because the decision-making process may be impaired by the drugs, which increases the chance of getting an STD like syphilis and HIV. Bisexual males and MSM like B and L in diagram I, have a higher chance of getting HIV and syphilis.

The new estimates of HIV incidence suggest that on average, a new HIV infection occurs every 9.5 minutes in the Unites States (Hall Hi et al, JAMA 2008) and AIDS related deaths occur roughly every 33 minutes. The dynamics of STD/HIV infection with the chain of transmission as shown in the diagrams I and II is a snapshot of the spread of HIV/AIDS epidemic and occurs around the clock daily. The vulnerable and those not ready to change or modify their sex behavior are waiting to join the chain of infection, transmission, disease and death from HIV/AIDS and other STDs if we do not improve the prevention and control measures.

Unprotected sex with someone who has STD/HIV is the final common pathway for sexual transmission of STD/HIV. However, I have noted from the dynamics of STD/HIV infection, the fact that, the infection and spread of STD/HIV involves a process of five main epidemiologic and behavior patterns leading to that common pathway. These five main epidemiologic and behavior patterns overlap but could independently make it easier for sex partners to be infected and spread STD/HIV to other sex partners, and occur in all sexual lifestyles of heterosexuals, bisexuals, transgenders and homosexuals. The five main patterns of infection and the spread of STD/HIV are:

1. Anonymous sex partner networks. Examples from diagram I are sex partners B, R and U1-U3, H and M1-M3. And from diagram II are Q and S1-S4.

2. New sex partner syndrome. This pattern makes persons like C capable of spreading HIV infection to new sex partners like G in diagram II

3. Old sex partner syndrome. This is the reason why persons like B can spread HIV to persons who behave like A in diagram I

4. Multiple simultaneous sex partners in open and polygamy sexual relationships, whereby, both sex partners have multiple other sex partners or one of the sex partners in a "stable sexual relationship" has one or more other sex partners. Example from diagram I is sex partners B and H. And example from diagram II is sex partners E and W.

5. Sex with a previous known HIV positive person who does not disclose HIV positive status. There is the lack of effective active surveillance system to inform sex partners of a previous HIV positive persons, about sexual contact to HIV until the previous HIV positive person test positive for some of the STDs like chlamydia, gonorrhea and syphilis. Therefore, persons who do not disclose their HIV status

are secretly infecting sex partners who don't check for a proof of HIV test results before having sex. This pattern has contributed to continuous spread of HIV especially, among MSM and bisexual sex partners. Example is a spread of HIV from B to J, L, H,R and A in diagram I.

There is not much done by the ongoing STD/HIV prevention efforts to recognize and reduce these five patterns of infection and spread of STD/HIV. Therefore, one person in five (approximately 21%) people infected with HIV in U.S. do not know that they have HIV infection and will spread HIV to other sex partners. These five main patterns may be responsible for the late diagnosis AIDS in about one person in three (approximately 36%) people diagnosed for new HIV infection.

Persons who knowingly or unknowingly get involved in any of these five patterns have a very high chance of getting STDs and HIV/AIDS.

The estimated life time cost of HIV treatment of a person in U.S. is approximately $355,000 by estimates for 2006. It is therefore essential for public health programs to work with the communities and explain these patterns to people and initiate projects and research to prevent and control these five main patterns which add a huge financial cost and human suffering to countries economic problems.

The public health system cannot just wait for people to test positive for HIV and then generate a high HIV positive rate to get grants and money for treatment. It is costly.

Rather, public health programs should work to reduce the high rates of STDs and HIV infection in the communities they serve. The families and people in the communities must participate in public health programs and modify behaviors to help reduce high rates of STD/HIV.

The cost of HIV care is expensive and it is every persons responsibility to modify sexual lifestyles and drug use behaviors to prevent it.

Therefore, all known HIV positive persons must disclose HIV positive status to sex partner before sex and always use condoms to protect themselves from infections and protect the sex partners from HIV and other STDs. Any reasons given to avoid using condoms will continue to add unecessary cost to their health care and the care of their sex partners and other persons in the chain of STD/HIV infections. A cost that is directly or indirectly paid by the general public and the government to keep HIV positive persons alive.

A good quality time can be spent with people and explain the dynamics of STD/HIV infection and the use of protection method "ATBC" as part of our efforts to prevent STD/HIV and the added cost of care.

Doctors, nurses, HIV epidemiologist and STD/HIV disease intervention specialist, health behavior scientist and all public health workers involved in STD/HIV disease prevention and control must use the pattern of STD/HIV infection and the spread within their communities to initiate programs that will educate people to know how to protect themselves from those spreading STD/HIV by sexual transmission. Intervention programs should increase STD/HIV transmission prevention and HIV treatment monitoring knowledge and compliance by known HIV positive persons.

HIV positive persons must know that low CD4 count increases the chance of suffering from opportunistic infections and early death. They should take HIV medications to reduce the viral load and decrease perinatal HIV transmission to babies and sexual transmission of HIV to sex partners.

Sex partners must be given the chance to know HIV status and properly and consistently use condoms for protection. They must be notified of sexual exposure to HIV, early testing for HIV and linkage of those who test positive to HIV medical care and early treatment so that, they do not suffer from the consequences of late diagnosis of HIV/AID.

When a person knows of HIV positive status early and continue to see a doctor every three months and then begin HIV medication treatment at the time they need them, they are able to lower the HIV viral load and maintain good levels of CD4 count and live healthier and longer life than those who are diagnosed late to have a worsen HIV progression to AIDS.

Intervention programs to facilitate HIV medication treatment for many HIV positive persons or universal HIV treatment and early treatment of STDs such as directly observe therapy (DOT) to sex partners must be implemented to interrupt transmission of STD/HIV by reducing the number of active carriers of high infectious load of HIV.

Protection of the general public such as HIV negative sex partner must include messages of testing a sex partner for HIV and STDs before sexual relationship to avoid coming into sexual contact with HIV from the pattern of ongoing infections and spread of STD/HIV.

Individual HIV prevention action plan to avoid the five patterns of infection and spread of STD/HIV must be encouraged and supported by communities all over the world.

The dynamics of STD/HIV infection as explained from diagram I and II requires that all public health departments must have well trained carrier professionals of STD/HIV epidemiologist, disease intervention specialist, health educators and health behavior scientist to team up with physicians and nurses and initiate cost-effective and efficient STD/HIV disease investigations and behavior modification for efficient prevention of the spread of STD/HIV. Appropriate referral to mental health, pyschiatrics and drug rehabilitation centers for persons with significant deviant uncontrollable STD/HIV transmission behaviors that makes a known STD/HIV positive person a significant risk for the spread of STD/HIV to other individuals and the community should always be considered and implemented whenever it becomes necessary. Other known persons affected by positive HIV results may benefit from such referrals and rehabilitation to help them cope with the problems associated with living with HIV and comply with HIV/AIDS treatment by their physicians.

For every known case of STD/HIV, there are at least two other possible locatable exposed sex partners who will benefit from testing and treatment and thus, an excellent disease investigation skills and committed personnel with passion to help people and the community to prevent infectious STD/HIV are needed. Unfortunate, STD/HIV disease investigation has not yet been given its due respect with adequate number and team of professionals that will work with individuals and the community to help control STD/HIV epidemic, provide good STD/HIV knowledge and practical individualized prevention information to our youth and young adults to protect themselves from living with HIV for the remaining part of their lives.

There is the need and responsibility by countries and county health departments to train more STD/HIV professionals to help control the HIV epidemic but we have not done much and have few STD/

HIV workers in the community to do disease investigation for the over burden STD/HIV epidemic. Thus, what tends to happen is that, people who have sex with anonymous sex partners, ignore to protect themselves from STD/HIV and have not been doing regular testing for HIV do not get the chance to be notified and then benefit from early diagnosis of HIV infection until they are very sick and diagnosed with AIDS. Be careful to take the necessary steps to protect yourself and do regular testing with your sex partner and prevent getting HIV/AIDS.

Behavior modification to prevent STD/HIV should be a continuous effort and a process, if a person does not want to be part of the chain of transmission, infection and re-infection by STD/HIV and its associate complications and financial burden. Therefore anytime a person presents at STD and HIV clinic or testing site, emergency room, urgent care centers and other health care facilities where STD/HIV test is available, there is the opportunity to spend a few minutes to discuss individual risk of HIV infection during pre-test counseling and the posting of the STD/HIV test results (post-test counseling). STD/HIV test counselors should not just rush persons through the test for the sake of just testing more people, rather it is unique opportunity to use the persons STD/HIV risk to assess individualized HIV risk and briefly discuss action steps to modify risk behavior with practical information that will help the person to avoid coming into contact with HIV infection.

Testing for STD/HIV presents a good opportunity to discuss primary prevention of "ATBC" without being judgmental and then offer hope to those who test HIV positive with information about the benefit of early HIV diagnosis and compliance with early follow up monitoring of HIV and immune system at the HIV clinic by physicians. Prevention of infections and proper use of condoms always for self-protection, protection of sex partner and prevention of transmission and re-infection with possible resistant HIV from other HIV positive persons should be discussed. The fact that compliance with HIV monitoring and treatment with HIV medications (also known as HAART) will prevent AIDS over many years must be mention to give the newly diagnosed HIV positive person a hope of care and support by the medical system. Proper linkage to HIV clinic, case manager and mental health counselors- whenever necessary, must be done to help HIV positive person to modify behavior and benefit from treatment.

Provision of condoms to newly diagnosed HIV positive persons should be part of the post-test counseling and immediate need of behavior modification to help the person to stay healthy and prevent the complication that could be imposed by additional STD like syphilis, hepatitis C and B and herpes simplex infection. Discussion of reduction of number of sex partners, informing sex partners of HIV positive status and giving sex partners the chance to test for HIV and benefit from early treatment is essential before the HIV positive person leaves the testing site. Those who used to donate blood and plasma must be made aware that they cannot do it anymore. Others who use syringes and needles for intravenous drug injections and those who abuse drugs like alcohols and methamphetamine will benefit from early referral to rehab centers to help them to change or modify behavior so that they do not continue to spread HIV. Drug rehab will help them to reduce their chance of complications of other infections in addition to the HIV because of the suppressed immune system. HIV testing centers and clinics should not forget rehab referrals for female and male sex escorts and prostitutes who will be ready to modify or quit their behavior to prevent spreading HIV to other people in the community.

Honest sex partners cannot hide STD/HIV test results. Commitment to only one sex partner who has no STD/HIV and has committed to only you in a monogamous sexual relationship is the key to avoid getting an STD/HIV infection. If possible, I wish everyone should consider getting married and make sure this happens.

3

STD/HIV treatment behavior

A personal plan for STD/HIV behavior modification is essential for STD prevention and to stop the spread of infection. It is very important that a person who has a sexually transmitted disease get treatment as quickly as possible together with the sex partner(s). For example, when a person is diagnosed with gonorrhea or chlamydia, the sex partner(s) within the last two to three months or the last sex partner must be treated. If a person has syphilis, the sex partners within the past year should be interviewed and treated as directed by the doctor and STD/HIV public health worker.

It is advisable that a person treated for STD should not have sex with the sex partner until both the person and the sex partner have completed taking all the medications. When a person is treated for gonorrhea or chlamydia, it is advised that the person wait for one more week to get complete healing before the next sexual activity.

People who are not able to wait for one week before the next sexual activity are encouraged to use condoms consistently during the week after completion of treatment to ensure complete healing and prevent recurrence or complications especially in women.

Complete treatment of all sex partners for STDs

Every person is encouraged to help prevent the spread of STDs and HIV. It is very important for people to help doctors and public health workers to make quick decisions to prevent the spread of STD/HIV by providing good information about the sex partner. That disclosure gives other people the chance to get tested and receive medical treatment to stop them from unknowingly spreading STD/HIV. Health care workers keep all testing, sex partners, and treatment information confidential because they cannot tell for sure who might have given a person STD/HIV. No health worker will give out sex partner information unless a person gives a health worker the permission to reveal the name to the sex partner. STD/HIV positive patients who want to discuss testing, treatment, and prevention with their sex partner are encouraged to do so.

Let us care for each other. People are encouraged to make sure that their sex partners have been treated by asking them for the treatment papers or medication bottles. No one can protect a person from STD/HIV unless that person actively participates in the process of protecting himself or herself. It is not a matter of trust in this case but a matter of making sure that the right thing is done because people may say that they have taken the medication, but it may not be the right medication for the specific STD. Or the person may have two infections but has taken medication for only one of them.

Some people may say that they have been treated, but that information may not be true or partially true because they have not completed taking their medications and can give back the infection to their sex partner (in other words, re-infect the sex partner). There are other people who will test and will not even go for their test results and will continue to spread STD/HIV infection. It is important to know the test results and get treatment to avoid complications especially the deadly complications of HIV/AIDS.

The HIV epidemic in African American women and men who have sex with men is increasing. Early treatment of STDs in populations of African American women and men who have sex with men is vital to the control of STD/HIV since it is a fact that having other STDs increases the chance of getting HIV infection after sex with an HIV-infected person.

Every person and especially every young person 15–24 years of age are encouraged to abstain from sex at the time of untreated STD/HIV and before marriage to avoid unnecessary suffering from HIV/AIDS. People who are not ready to abstain from sex before marriage are encouraged to consider it. If they are not ready to practice abstinence, they should consider protecting themselves by using condoms to avoid passing on infectious deadly diseases like HIV to innocent people especially if they have been diagnosed and are receiving medical treatment for STD/HIV. This will protect others from undue suffering.

In case a person knows that he or she has a deadly HIV infection and passes it on to innocent people, he or she is considered to have knowingly attempted to commit murder under the law of the land. It is not good for us to kill someone with HIV infection.

Complete treatment for STDs is necessary to avoid complications.

Complete treatment means both sex partners have finished taking all the medications as directed by the doctor. It helps to prevent getting the infection back (re-infection), getting PID, and having infertility.

STD/HIV treatment of pregnant patients

All pregnant patients are required to test for STDs especially HIV, chlamydia, gonorrhea, syphilis, and hepatitis B. Additional tests for other STDs are required based on the lifestyle of the pregnant woman and her sex partner(s).

For all pregnant women infected with an STD, a follow-up test for cure is recommended to be done by the doctor to make sure the infection is gone so that the baby does not get the infection especially at the time of birth. Gonorrhea and chlamydia can infect the eyes of the baby at the time of birth in case a pregnant woman is not cured before the baby is born.

It will be good for pregnant women to request that their doctors give them medication prescriptions for their husbands or sex partners at the same time to make sure that they are treated early and the baby protected. Unfortunately, many women especially the adolescent pregnant women do not know where the baby's father can be found, but it is important that arrangement is made with the health worker to make sure that the baby's father gets tested and medical treatment for the STD given, even if there is no more sexual relationship going on. In case the man is not treated like the sex partner B in diagram I of chapter two, and the sexual relationship is renewed, the pregnant woman, like sex partner H, is likely to get the STD again and may pass it on to the baby. This is also an example of old sex partner syndrome.

Treatment of babies and children up to age fourteen who get exposed to STDs is not discussed in this book. A doctor must be consulted for management of such a diagnosis.

Every pregnant woman is encouraged to do HIV testing and follow up the test results throughout the pregnancy and at the time of delivery. This is very important because HIV medications called zidovudine (ZDV) and nevirapine can be given to the HIV positive pregnant woman after the first thirteen weeks of pregnancy or at the time of delivery. Then preventive HIV medications are given to the baby for the first six to fourteen weeks after birth to protect the baby from getting HIV infection. HIV positive women should not breastfeed the baby because it has been found to cause transmission (14 percent risk of transmission) of HIV infection to the baby.

The transfer of HIV infection from mother to a child at time of pregnancy, delivery, and through breastfeeding is called vertical transmission of HIV infection. It is good for a woman to test before and during pregnancy and at the time of labor and delivery. If the woman is HIV positive, she should follow up with a doctor for treatment with zidovudine or nevirapine to prevent vertical transmission of STD/HIV.

Research has shown that medications other than zidovudine (ZDV) may be as effective in preventing vertical transmission. Medication such as nevirapine has several beneficial effects. It can cross the placenta and get to the baby. It is present in high concentrations of more than 60 percent of plasma levels in breast milk. Furthermore, studies have demonstrated that nevirapine is 47 percent more effective than ZDV in decreasing HIV transmission and less expensive (World Health Organization 2003, Guay 1999, Connor 1994, Stinger 1999).

Pregnant women who test positive may protect their newborns from HIV with ZDV or nevirapine even in poor African and developing countries. Studies demonstrate that ZDV given to the mother during pregnancy and delivery and to newborn infants reduces HIV transmission rates by 70 percent (Bryson 1996, Bulterys 1998, Ramos 2000).

The increase in HIV infection among women of childbearing age increases the potential health risks to these women, their children, and society in general (Tabi and Frimpong 2003). Globally, 20% of the HIV infections occur in 15-25-years-olds and existing cases (seroprevalence) among pregnant African women increased from 10 to 40% in the last decade in the urban areas (Joint UN Programme on HIV/AIDS 2002).

Prophylaxis and HIV risk reduction of infants in Africa and developing countries

The crude birth and fertility rates of most African countries are high. The greater proportion of the population is under fifteen years old (Tabi and Frimpong 2003). A greater percentage of adults living with HIV are women in their reproductive years. This poses a substantial potential risk for vertical transmission of infection from mother to child in African countries. The route of transmission of the virus to women in African countries is mainly through heterosexual intercourse (the sexual relationship between a man and a woman) (Tabi and Frimpong 2003). Therefore, prevention of vertical transmission of HIV would be a cost-effective measure of HIV prevention in developing countries. Unfortunately, the use of ZDV for control of vertical transmission of

HIV is not readily available in Africa and some developing countries (Tabi and Frimpong 2003).

Approximately 14 percent of vertical transmission of HIV is through breast milk (Nduati 2000). Breastfeeding should not be done if the mother is HIV infected (Tabi and Frimpong 2003). Except in situations where it has been confirmed by HIV test that the baby is already HIV positive. Advocating the use of formula feeding by HIV-infected mothers in most African countries, particularly among women in rural areas, requires the cost-effective provision of formula feeds and access to a clean water supply, which may not be available.

The cost of exclusive milk formula feeding of a baby for 6 months is approximately $750 to $1000. The use of Enfamil or similac will cost about $ 1500-2000 for 12 months of milk formula feeding of new born baby in U.S. (source: http://www.thelaboroflove.com) but the price can be lower in other parts of the world. Financing exclusive milk formula and milk products feeding of babies born to HIV positive mothers in the developing countries to prevent vertical transmission of HIV in breast milk from HIV positive mother to a new born baby in areas of countries where potable drinking water is made available is very important. It may be a viable option to be considered by various NGOs, governments and other health care agencies in developing countries because breast milk has 14% risk of transmission of HIV from infected mother to a baby.

Financing exclusive milk formula feeding to prevent vertical transmission of HIV to babies in developing countries may be cost-effective compare to the cost of human suffering from the complications of AIDS, the cost of medical treatment of a child infected with HIV/AIDS and treatment of the opportunistic infections over many years before death from HIV/AIDS.

Few women in Africa and other developing countries have the luxury of bottle-feeding. Access to clean water would allow HIV-infected women to use formula milk products to feed their children rather than breast milk. It would also reduce the acquisition of other infectious diseases that affect the health of both parents and the child. Overcoming these limitations is essential to reducing HIV infection and transmission of infants in Africa and developing countries (Tabi and Frimpong 2003).

The concomitant high fertility and high HIV infection rates increase the risk of vertical HIV transmission and infection in newborns and children. The importance of understanding the global effect of HIV infection among women is crucial to developing interventions to meet the challenges passed by this devastating disease on the health of the vulnerable populations worldwide and particularly in Africa. Equally important is the effect of HIV deaths on families, social systems, and national economic growth and development (Tabi and Frimpong 2003).

Governments in Africa and other developing countries should continuously initiate programs that make prophylactic HIV medications like zidovudine and nevirapine as well as formula feeds available and accessible to babies of HIV-infected mothers to prevent transmission of HIV from mothers to infants after they are born. Such programs could be similar to those implemented in the Western developed countries like the U.S. for pregnant women from low-income families. Political will and the involvement of non-governmental organizations (NGOs) can make such projects for HIV-infected mothers and their infants possible.

I believe the extended family systems in Africa and developing countries will make it easy for family members to adopt infants and children who do not contract HIV infection from their HIV-infected mothers before and after the death of their HIV-infected mothers. The U.S. President's Emergency Plan for AIDS Relief (PEPFAR) initiated in 2003 for Africa and other developing countries is a good example of political will at a time of an infectious disease epidemic to reduce the risk of HIV infection in countries where such efforts are needed most. Governments in such countries can actively complement such efforts to protect infants from HIV infection.

4

STD/HIV prevention action plan

Most people who do not have an STD/HIV prevention action plan are dying from HIV infection. Therefore, everybody must have an STD/HIV prevention action plan, talk openly to the sex partner about it, and consistently follow the action plan.

Why is it so important to consistently maintain an individual STD/HIV prevention action plan? The people who ignore it are getting a deadly HIV infection that has no cure. Let us take a look at the statistics in a literature review and the significance of STD/HIV infection and the use of protective measures.

Statistical facts of STD/HIV prevention

According to CDC recommendations and reports in *Morbidity and Mortality Weekly Report (MMWR* 2006), when used consistently and correctly, male latex condoms are highly effective in preventing the sexual transmission of HIV infection. HIV negative partners in heterosexual relationships with HIV positive sex partner (in other words, HIV serodiscordant sexual relationship) in which condoms were consistently used were 80 percent less likely to become HIV infected compared with people in similar relationships in which condoms were not used and can reduce the risk of other STDs, including chlamydia, gonorrhea, and trichomoniasis, and might reduce the risk of developing pelvic inflammatory diseases (Kimberly 2006, Holmes 2004, Ness 2004).

Condom use might reduce the risk for herpes simplex virus-2 (HSV-2) (Wald 2005, Wald 2001) and HPV-associated diseases (such as genital warts and cancer of the cervix) (Kimberly 2006, Manhart 2002). One recent follow-up study among newly sexually active college women demonstrated that consistent condom use was associated with a 70 percent reduction in risk for HPV transmission (Kimberly 2006, Winer 2006). Latex condoms were used in these studies.

The female condoms when used consistently and correctly may substantially reduce the risk for STDs (World Health Organization 2003, French 2003). Limited numbers of clinical studies have evaluated the efficacy of female condoms in providing protection from STDs, including HIV (Kimberly 2006, French 2003).

County, district, and state health departments can initiate STD/HIV prevention action plans in addition to encouraging individual personal prevention plans to reduce STDs in the community.

For instance, the STD Field Operations of the Duval County Health Department in Jacksonville, Florida, have demonstrated by intervention study that the implementation of a doctor's written protocol of field treatment of chlamydia and gonorrhea STD through a process of directly observed therapy (DOT), sex partner contact investigations, and counseling can reduce existing cases of chlamydia and gonorrhea in the community and ensures increased rates of early treatment intervention.

The study found that a field-based, field worker delivered directly observed therapy (DOT) in 2006 compared to pre-DOT in 2003 resulted in the treatment and interview of 121 percent more chlamydia and gonorrhea patients, testing and treatment of 72 percent more sexual partners in 2004, with 25 percent less disease intervention specialists in 2004. A reduction in the percentage of women who had chlamydia (2.5 percent) and gonorrhea (6.5 percent) cases per 100,000 population in the age group 15–24 years was noted for the three-year period from 2004 to 2006. Most significantly, the percentage of cases treated within fourteen days of testing "early secondary intervention" for chlamydia and gonorrhea improved from 63 percent during the first six months of 2003 to 91 percent for gonorrhea and 80 percent for chlamydia for the first six months of 2004, attesting to the effectiveness of DOT on a target risk group for the interruption of the chlamydia and gonorrhea transmission from one sex partner to the other (Sands 2007, DOT data reference).

Early treatment intervention for chlamydia and gonorrhea will most likely be a significant advantage of DOT for control of both STDs. DOT may decrease the duration of infection by increasing the number of people cured within a shorter time of diagnosis and could decrease the rate of existing cases and decrease the continuous spread of chlamydia and gonorrhea by those who would otherwise refuse to go back to the doctor's office for their test results and treatment because of lack of transportation or money to pay for their medical expenses. Maybe it can help to reduce the number of new cases of chlamydia and gonorrhea as the existing cases in the community are treated early.

DOT offers the advantage of counseling sex partners together with their consent at their convenience and in the privacy of their home or in the health department satellite offices. It also offers the assurance that since sex partners did not test before they started to have sex they cannot blame each other and gives them the opportunity to openly discuss and adopt new preventive measures to protect each other. The sex partners who want to commit to each other usually have no problem with having STD/HIV prevention counseling together, getting DOT, and discussing STD/HIV protection of each other. Again, honest sex partners cannot hide STD/HIV test results.

The CDC has summarized the prevention of STD/HIV at its Web site http://cdc.gov/hiv/topics/basic/#prevention/ as ABC: Abstinence, Be faithful and Condoms usage as the basic primary prevention from STD/HIV. Studies in Uganda, Africa, using the acronym "ABC" for STD/HIV prevention supported by the government and public health staff has remarkably reduced prevalence of HIV in the country.

Uganda's HIV prevention campaign effort appears to have reduced the prevalence rate of HIV from 14 percent in the early 1990s to 8.3 percent in 2000 (Avert 2001, World Development Indicators Database 2000). The Uganda HIV prevention program has employed strong political will with support from the president downward, with a well-defined national plan, and community involvement with open publicity in health education campaigns (Tabi and Frimpong 2003).

We can learn from this literature review that a combination of programs can reduce existing cases of STD/HIV. These programs include STD/HIV health education to increase the knowledge about STD/HIV, discussions to enable people to use primary prevention methods like abstinence, being faithful to one sex partner and condoms (ABC) as well as the efficient STD investigation and the use of early secondary prevention (DOT by STD health workers to help people to initiate and maintain a modified STD/HIV risk reduction behavior).

Act now to prevent STD/HIV infections

Why do we need to act now to reduce the prevalence of STD/HIV especially in the youth and young adults? Because STD/HIV infection is not a problem in Africa alone though HIV is spreading at a faster rate in that continent. Similar statistics are seen all over the world. The statistics of STD/HIV infections in the U.S. are overwhelming and can be improved. Consider this:

1. Each year 19 million new STD cases are diagnosed, half of them (9.5 million) occur in the youth and young adults 15–24 years by CDC estimates. This implies that STD is common in the youth and young adults, who need to take STD/HIV prevention action seriously.

2. In 2004, the CDC estimated that 4,883 youth ages 13–24 from thirty-three states in the U.S. have HIV/AIDS (that's 13 percent of all new cases) (CDC, Healthy Youth). Approximately one million people in the U.S. are living with HIV/AIDS, and one quarter of them do not know they have it. It is better for people to test at least once yearly and

benefit from the treatment with highly active antiretroviral therapy (HAART), which has slowed the HIV progression to AIDS since 1996. Thus, more HIV positive patients are living longer and are more likely to infect other people. The cost of caring for more HIV positive patients could be a burden on the government and the community. Therefore it is important for people to learn and adopt and maintain the primary prevention "ATBC" of STD/HIV.

3. African Americans make up 13 percent of the U.S. population but account for 49 percent of HIV/AIDS cases. Data from thirty-three states indicated that African American men account for 41 percent of cases in all men. African American women make up 64 percent of all women in 2005, and 104 out of 166 new cases (66 percent) in children are African American children. In 2005, about half (49 percent) of the people diagnosed with HIV/AIDS were blacks (CDC, HIV/AIDS and African Americans). According to the CDC, African Americans who are diagnosed with HIV/AIDS do not live long because of poverty. HIV/AIDS is becoming the leading cause of death in the African American population.

4. In 2000, 13 percent of all pregnancies (831,000) occurred in the age group 15–19 (CDC, Healthy Youth). This means that approximately 831,000 sexually active young women age 15–19 and approximately 831,000 babies (infants) could be exposed to STD/HIV in a year depending on the number of the male sex partners who have STD/HIV. Indeed, most chlamydia and gonorrhea cases in women are diagnosed during routine testing for STDs at the time of

pregnancy and Pap smear screening. Testing women for STD/HIV helps to find the male sex partners who may have STD/HIV. Male sex partners who may test positive for chlamydia or gonorrhea or both but have no symptoms could otherwise miss testing, diagnosis, and treatment and will continue to spread STDs within the community. Testing females for STD/HIV during pregnancy and Pap smear is a good means of finding STD and HIV in the community since most men are often reluctant to test unless they have signs and symptoms of chlamydia and gonorrhea or have a penile sore.

5. By 2005, 47 percent of all high school students were sexually active, and 14 percent have more than four sex partners. Also, 34 percent of sexually active high school students did not use a condom during their last sexual intercourse. In 2002, 3 percent of males aged 15–19 had anal sex (sex in the "butt") with a male. We know that HIV infection is increasing in the age group of those 15–24 years especially in men who have sex with men (MSM) (CDC, Healthy Youth).

6. Men who have sex with men make up 68 percent of all men living with HIV in 2005 though they account for 5 percent to 7 percent of all men, and 46 percent of African America men who are MSM have HIV (CDC, HIV/AIDS and Men Who Have Sex with Men). This high proportion of HIV among African American men who have sex with men increases the burden of the rise of HIV infection among African American women since it has been found that some of these men are having sex with both men and

women (they are bisexual) and conceal their sexual identity "down low" from their female sex partners. Eventually they pass on the HIV infection to their female sex partners.

7. New cases of HIV/AIDS in MSM in 2005 were 11 percent more than number of cases in 2001 (CDC, HIV/AIDS and Men Who Have Sex with Men). This is an indication that HIV/AIDS continues to increase in men who have sex with men, though at a slower rate compared to the period of 1981 to 1995.

This number of cases will continue to increase as HIV patients live longer on HIV medications if we do not encourage individualized STD/HIV prevention action plans among MSM in addition to the public health prevention efforts by health services providers, government, and non-governmental organizations.

More new cases of HIV will add to the existing cases of those living with HIV infection, as patients take HIV medications to reduce the HIV/AIDS death rate as patients. More people within the community are going to live with HIV infection if we don't do much more active STD/HIV prevention action. Let us encourage our children to adopt behaviors that will not make them live with HIV infection for the rest of their lives since HIV has no vaccine for prevention and no cure at this time.

The only way we can reduce the rate of new cases (incidence) and existing cases (prevalence) of HIV is to reduce the risk factors (these are behaviors that will make people get STD/HIV infection). Therefore, we should encourage behaviors that will not make people get HIV infection. Sexual contact between someone who has STD/HIV and a person who has no STD/HIV must be reduced and avoided. This will be one of the most efficient ways to reduce new HIV infections. Thus, abstinence and testing together with your partner to know the test results for STD/HIV before sex and using protective male or female condoms, even when the results of the HIV tests are negative because of the window period of three to six months and Be faithful to one sex partner such as marriage (monogamy) - all these prevention measures known as "ATBC"- will be good behaviors to avoid sexual contact, exposure, and HIV infection.

According to CDC estimates, AIDS has been diagnosed in half a million MSM, and 300,000 MSM diagnosed with AIDS have died. People have freedom to choose behaviors they want, but this high amount of suffering and death could be avoided with consistent, individualized STD/HIV prevention action. People should not choose behaviors that will lead to suffering and death from HIV/AIDS. It is a very sad experience to see and take care of someone suffering and dying from HIV/AIDS and its complications.

In communities such as in Africa where people get HIV infection mainly from a man having sex with a woman, a high number of children are at risk of getting HIV infection within the first year of life and becoming orphans early in life as their parents die from HIV infection. For example, the estimated number of children alive who have lost one or both parents to AIDS in Africa was 11 million by 2001 (Tabi and Frimpong 2003, Joint UN Programme 2002). Let's envision the kind of life and the socioeconomic burden these children will experience without the guidance and help from their natural parents to achieve their full potential in life.

Even though more testing for HIV is being done now, if the primary prevention method "ABC" is serious adopted and done actively, the new cases of HIV will decrease significantly even in the setting of more testing. For public health infectious disease screening test, there is the observation that you will find more cases when you do more testing and or use more accurate test. This is more applicable to old existing cases before initiating a prevention plan. When people are maintaining a prevention plan of ABC for HIV prevention, we should not find more new HIV infections as reported by CDC for 2006 because there will be decrease in the number of new sexual exposure to HIV infections and decrease in number of existing cases of HIV as those who have HIV infection for many years die or protect their sex partners.

HIV can be limited to only very high risk group who have already got it and the number of new cases stabilize or decrease if the very high risk group of HIV positive persons and their sex partners always maintain the ABC prevention plan for HIV. For example, new cases of SARS reduced and eliminated from parts of China when all the people who came into contact with those who had SARS or could have it, protected themselves with a mask to avoid coming into contact with the infection. Similar method of prevention by consistent and proper use of condoms always by those who stubbornly refused to keep sex to only one sex partner and those who know their HIV positive status may protect people from HIV and other STDs. It is better to test together and protect a sex partner than to secretly kill a sex partner with HIV infection.

Unfortunately, unprotected sex has been a way for some people to show their love to persons who are not their husband or wife and whose HIV test results is not known. People are making a mistake of having such unprotected sex even to their death with HIV/AIDS. Therefore, it makes it difficult to decrease HIV infection. CDC cited poverty, STDs, unprotected sex, and sex in exchange for money as the reasons for this increase of new HIV infections.

Globally, the STD and HIV prevention action should involve individual action plans, family, government, community-based organizations (CBO), community leaders, non-governmental organizations, (NGO) and health care facilities like hospitals, clinics, and public health services. For instance, in Sub-Saharan Africa, Botswana had the highest number of people living with HIV by the year 2000. Approximately 36 percent of the adult population was estimated to be infected with HIV by a World Health Organization (WHO) HIV/AIDS epidemiological update. Aggressive programs for behavior change, condom promotion, voluntary HIV counseling and testing, and blood transfusion safety have lowered existing cases. Similar efforts in several Sub-Saharan African countries have slowed the spread of HIV infection for the past decade.

Uganda was among the nations with the highest HIV infection rates in the 1990s, but the government aggressively pursued the "ABC" prevention action to decrease the overall adult HIV infection rate from 14 percent to 8 percent. In Musaka, Uganda, the HIV cases among females age 20–24 decreased from 20.9 percent during 1989–1990 to 13.8 percent during 1996–1997.

In Lusaka, Zambia, HIV cases among females age 15–19 years attending prenatal clinics decreased from 27 percent in 1993 to 17 percent in 1998. In West Africa, Senegal has maintained prevalence of approximately 2 percent by the same efforts as Uganda by 2000 and by regulating commercial sex workers, intensive condom promotion, and treatment of STDs and community mobilization reported by WHO HIV/AIDS epidemiological update.

The treatment of HIV is necessary to prevent undue suffering and to preserve human dignity especially in babies up to one year of age (infants) and children. Maternal plasma HIV viral load (that is, the approximate amount of HIV in the blood) is the most important risk factor associated with mother-to-infant HIV transmission (Stringer 1999, Garcia 1999). When the treatment reduces the amount of the HIV in the blood (viral load), there is significant reduction in the chances of passing on the HIV infection to a sex partner and from an HIV positive pregnant mother to the infant. Treatment of HIV-infected pregnant women reduces the chance of vertical transmission of HIV to the baby.

The cost of HIV infection continues to affect the individual budget plans and the government financial resources since the disease affects the socioeconomic development of the country when the young productive individuals become less productive and cannot work to support the economy. Therefore an STD/HIV prevention action plan is necessary for socioeconomic development of a country and must be taken serious. In U.S., Ryan White Program is helping to pay for the medical expenses of thousands of HIV/AIDS patients who qualify for government assistance, to get medical treatment and supportive services. The U.S. President's Emergency Plan for AIDS Relief (PEPFAR) has continued to subsidize HIV medical treatment for many African countries since 2003.

In Brazil, reported HIV related deaths declined from 22 per 100,000 in 1995 to approximately 15 per 100,000 people infected with HIV in 1999 by government policy to provide universal free access to HIV medical treatment with highly active antiretroviral therapy (HAART). These are very good examples of HIV prevention action plans by governments since treatment reduces viral load and

HIV transmission rates especially from mother to baby and helps the mother to live longer and take care of the baby

In Africa where the male-to-female (heterosexual) mode of HIV infection is the most common means of infection, a strategy to counsel married couples about STD/HIV prevention must be made an important part of the initial marriage agreement. People must be encouraged to test before marriage and to do two HIV tests (at the beginning of the relationship and then six months later). This may help to prevent a person who has HIV infection during the window period of three to six months after infection when there is HIV infection but an undetectable amount in the blood for the available test to be positive, from passing HIV infection to the married partner.

HIV test in the window period of three months to six months from the time of exposure to HIV infection may be negative, but a person will have the HIV infection in the blood and pass it to the sex partner after the six-month period. Ideally anyone who is named by an HIV positive sex partner but who tested negative by the first test should be followed up by the public health services for a second HIV test six months after the first test. But because of lack of personnel, many public health services are not able to do it. In case the exposed HIV partner forgets or is not motivated to do a second HIV test because of fear of testing positive for HIV, such a person will then become a potential source of new spread of HIV infection to other sex partners and may be diagnosed late with AIDS and complications of many diseases.

Since HIV spreads mainly by heterosexual sex in developing countries, the females in Africa and other developing countries must be empowered to demand that a fiancé or sex partner test twice for HIV before marriage or sex with a male sex partner since the female has ten times the chance of getting HIV infection from a male partner compared to the spread of HIV infection from female to male.

PEPFAR, together with the CDC, Rwanda Zambia HIV research group (RZHRG), the Liverpool School of Tropical Medicine and other national and international partners have developed a recommendation for couples regarding HIV counseling and testing intervention. This recommendation is also applicable to sex partners and cohabiting or married couples. The group recommended that HIV prevention counselors should assist couples by doing the following:

1. Providing clear and accurate prevention messages tailored to the couple's lifestyle and reasons for seeking HIV testing and counseling services

2. Mitigating tension and diffusing blame

3. Dispelling myths about HIV transmission

4. Creating an environment that is safe for disclosure of HIV status among partners

5. Discussing options for disclosure of HIV status to the couple's children and thinking through the appropriate next steps for testing children, when necessary.

Individual sustained STD/HIV prevention action plan

Client-centered, individual lifestyle modification based on an STD/HIV prevention action plan is a necessity for every person especially the youth and young adults from the ages of fifteen to twenty-four and must be encouraged to reduce the STD/HIV epidemic. Let us remind each other about the STD/HIV prevention action plan and let us protect each other as shown here.

STD/HIV PREVENTION ACTION PLAN

STD and HIV/AIDS prevention depends on your decisions.

These prevention measures may help protect you:

1. Abstinence from sex.

When you decide to have sex, it is advised that:

1. You and your sex partner must test for STD and HIV and you see each others' results before you start having sex.

2. Using condoms for all sexual activities may help protect you.

3. Limiting your sexual activity in marriage to one partner who will limit sex to you only (monogamy) may help protect you.

4. Avoid sharing of needles, syringes and razors.

5. Avoid having sex at the time of drinking alcohol and intoxication with drugs like cocaine, heroin, and marijuana so that you don't make a mistake of having sex with someone who has STD/HIV.

6. Test for STD and HIV before and during pregnancy to protect the baby.

This model of a recommended STD/HIV prevention action plan is modified and summarized based on a literature search of STD prevention guidelines by CDC and a personal STD/HIV field investigation experience.

The real action for protection starts when a person who has abstained from sex decides to have sex. So abstinence is one step which has no risk of getting STD/HIV by sex. When a person decides to have sex then there is some level of risk of getting STD/HIV and that is when a person's ability to use objective risk reduction plan that avoid coming into contact with STD/HIV becomes very important. Testing before sex therefore becomes the most important first step to make informed decision to avoid sexual contact with an established STD/HIV infection. The other prevention steps depends on the character and decisions of sex partners to protect each other.

The most important STD/HIV prevention action that makes ABC prevention of HIV effective is testing for HIV infection together with your sex partner and verifying each others results before the beginning of sexual relationship and even before marriage and the use of condom always. Failure to verify sex partner's most recent HIV test results within the last 3 months (if possible, two test results within 3 to 6 months) as the first step and then maintaining the BC part of ABC (that is, Be faithful to limit sex to only one sex partner (monogamy) and use Condoms) always, is the driving force for the HIV epidemic when people change from abstinence to the point of beginning a sexual relationship.

The failure of people to test and verify their sex partner's HIV results before they begin sexual relationship has given many HIV positive persons who know or do not know their HIV positive status the chance to spread HIV infection. Remember that 21% (one person in five people) of those infected with HIV don't know it, and many people with HIV (36%, approximately one person in three people) are diagnosed late in their illness (CDC, Morbidity and Mortality Weekly Report (MMWR) 2006).

It is known from STD/HIV pretest counseling that most people are not able to use condoms always for sex even when they know that they have high risk behavior of getting STD/HIV. There is evidence that persons who know that their sex partners are already HIV positive are more likely to protect themselves with proper use of condoms always and if they chose to continue a stable relationship, they are eighty percent (80%) less likely to become HIV-infected compared with persons in similar relationships in which condoms were not used and can reduce the risk of other STDs (Kimberly AW, 2006). This means that the proper use of condoms consistently will reduce HIV infection by eighty percent (80%) when you have sex with a person who has HIV infection. But some people refuse to use it when they make a mistake to have sex with someone who is not committed to them as the only sex partner and they get STD/HIV infection.

Testing for HIV and verifying each others results before beginning a sexual relationship is a personal responsibility and a responsibility to the person we claim to love, the family, the government and the community. A lot of people made mistakes in the past and got HIV infection from already known HIV positive persons by not testing first before sexual relationship. It is our responsibility not to repeat such mistakes at present time of HIV epidemic and the availability of free and accessible test for STD/HIV.

Therefore remember ATBC: Abstinence, Test and verify for STD/HIV before sex, Be faithful to commit to one sex partner in

marriage (monogamy) and Condom use always may help protect you from STD/HIV.

HIV/AIDS epidemic has revealed that, a decision to have sex outside marriage is a serious mistake with a deadly consequences and more so, in situations where people begin a sexual relationship without testing for STD/HIV and verifying HIV results especially in high risk group such as men who have sex with men (MSM), bisexual men and people who have many sex partners and anonymous sex partners.

5

STD/HIV knowledge and health education

These are the fourteen sexually transmitted diseases (STDs) that a person can get by having sex with someone who has a sexually transmitted disease or HIV.

1. Gonorrhea

2. Chlamydia

3. Syphilis

4. Chancroid

5. Granuloma inguinale (donovanosis)

6. Lymphogranuloma venerum (LGV)

7. Hepatitis B infection

8. Hepatitis C infection

9. Genital herpes

10. Genital warts (condylomata acuminata)

11. Trichomoniasis ("tric")

12. Pediculosis pubis ("crabs")

13. Scabies

14. Human immunodeficiency virus (HIV) and acquired immunodeficiency syndrome (AIDS)

These are STDs infections caused by bacteria:

1. Gonorrhea

2. Chlamydia

3. Syphilis

4. Chancroid

5. Granuloma inguinale (donovanosis)

6. Lymphogranuloma venerum (LGV)

These STDs are caused by viruses:

1. Hepatitis B infection

2. Hepatitis C infection

3. Genital herpes

4. Genital warts (condylomata acuminata)

5. HIV/AIDS

These STDs are caused by parasites (worms and crabs):

1. Trichomoniasis ("tric")

2. Pediculosis pubis ("crabs")

3. Scabies

Let us discuss each of these STDs and improve our knowledge about the disease process and complications, diagnosis, treatment, and prevention. When we learn and get to understand the pain, suffering, and the financial burden of these diseases on our bodies, our family, the community, and the government, it will help us to modify our sex behavior and protect each other from STD/HIV.

Gonorrhea:

Gonorrhea is caused by bacteria called *Neisseria gonorrhoeae*. The CDC estimates published in the treatment guidelines for STDs in 2006 states that 600,000 new infections occur each year in the U.S.

How can a person get gonorrhea?

A person can get gonorrhea by having sex (any kind of sex) with a person who has gonorrhea.

[B] Symptoms and signs

How will I know that I have gonorrhea?

The symptoms and signs that will make you aware that you have gonorrhea differ for men and women, but in both cases there may be no signs or symptoms at all. Yet a person who has it will pass it on to the sex partner.

Most men will have a yellowish or whitish-yellow discharge within three to five days after having sex with a person who has it, burning pain on passing urine (dysuria), and sometimes bleeding from the sore created by the gonorrhea in the urine passage (urethra) of the penis.

A woman may show symptoms between five and thirty days of being exposed to a person who has it. A vaginal discharge different from the usual fluid that lubricates the vagina is noted, pain passing urine (dysuria), along with lower abdominal pain or discomfort.

A baby whose mother has gonorrhea can get gonorrhea on the eyes at the time of being born as the baby passes through the birth canal. Within three days of birth, the baby will have red eyes, discharge from the eyes, and the eyelids will stick together.

Those who have sex at other sites of the body will see similar discharges, sores or ulcers and sometimes bleeding from the sores in such body sites as the mouth and anus.

[B] Complications

What happens when a person is infected with gonorrhea?

The bacteria will cause a sore in the urine passage (urethra) of the penis, vagina and the cervix, mouth, throat, anus and the rectum ("the butt") depending on which part of the lining of the body (mucous membrane) is exposed at the time of sexual activity.

In women, the infection can spread to the womb (uterus), the tubes (fallopian tubes), ovary that produces the eggs (ova) needed for a baby to develop, and the supporting structures of the womb and the ovary. Complications will develop if gonorrhea is not detected and completely cured with treatment. The complications are blockage of the tubes, which will prevent the sperm from meeting the egg to form a baby. This process is called infertility. The other complications are collection of inflammatory fluid (pus) in the tubes and the ovary called tubo-ovarian abscess or pus in the pelvic area called pelvic abscess. The inflammation can spread to the covering of the intestine (peritoneum) in the pelvic area called pelvic peritonitis.

Complications in men are inflammation of the tube (epididymis) that stores the sperm called epididymitis, inflammation of the testes (orchitis). Inflammation of both the tubes and the testes can occur (epididymo-orchitis). The bacteria that cause gonorrhea can get into the blood and cause inflammation and swelling of the big joints of the body (causing septic arthritis or swelling of the joints in the body) especially the knee.

[B] Diagnosis

What test can I do to find out that I have gonorrhea?

See your doctor immediately or go to the public health clinic or a testing and treatment center. Some of the penile discharge, a swab of the throat, rectum (butt), and the cervix can be taken and examined under the microscope to find the bacteria that cause gonorrhea. The sample can be taken to the laboratory and the bacteria will be made to grow (culture) and be identified. A quick test of the urine by amplified GC or DNA probe can be done to diagnose gonorrhea infection.

Regular screening by Pap smears and especially when pregnant and testing together with your sex partner before having sex is always recommended.

[B] Treatment

How is gonorrhea treated?

A person who has gonorrhea may be treated with any of the following antibiotics: ceftriaxone 125mg or 250mg injection once, vantine 400mg by mouth once, cefixime 400mg by mouth once, ofloxacin 400mg by mouth once. Other medications are spectinomycin injection and levofloxacin by mouth.

The Centers for Disease Control and Prevention recommend that levofloxacin and ciprofloxacin should not be used to treat gonorrhea in men who have sex with men, those with a history of recent travel, or partners who have traveled to areas with resistant gonorrhea infections, infection in California and Hawaii or infection in communities with increased resistance of gonorrhea to levofloxacin and ciprofloxacin.

It is recommended that a person who has gonorrhea must get additional medication for treatment of chlamydia as well, if there was no test result to prove that there is no chlamydia infection, because it is common to find chlamydia in patients who have a positive test for gonorrhea (*MMWR* 2006). Complete and early treatment of gonorrhea may cure the infection without complications. Therefore, the treatment of all sex partners is necessary.

Chlamydia

Chlamydia infection is caused by a bacteria called *chlamydia trichomatis*.

An estimated 7.4 million new cases occur in the U.S. per year. Chlamydia in women is the most important cause of infection of the female genital tract affecting the cervix, uterus, and the fallopian tubes and sometimes the ovary where it is known as PID with associated complications of ectopic pregnancy and infertility. A screening test of all sexually active women up to the age of twenty-five is recommended as is screening of older women who have a new sex partner or multiple sex partners (U.S. Preventive Services Task Force, 2001). The benefits of chlamydia screening in women have been demonstrated in areas where screening programs have reduced both the high rate of existing infection (prevalence) and high rates of PID (Scholes 1996, Kamwenda 1996).

How can you get chlamydia?

A person can get chlamydia in the same way as gonorrhea by having sex with someone who has it. Chlamydia infection among people who have gonorrhea is common.

[B] Symptoms and signs

What happen when a person gets chlamydia infection?

Most people, especially women who have chlamydia do not have any symptoms or signs at all and are not aware that they have the sexually transmitted disease of chlamydia. They are therefore more likely to have PID, fallopian tube scarring, blockage and infertility, and ectopic pregnancy. Some people may have whitish discharge from the vagina, penis, and rectum and pain when urinating (dysuria), pain on having sex (dyspareunia), and abnormal vaginal bleeding. Chlamydia infection can also occur in the throat of a person who has sex in the mouth and in the rectum of men who have sex with other men.

[B] Diagnosis

How will I know that I have chlamydia?

Chlamydia is diagnosed by testing and culture of the discharge with a swab from the vagina and cervix, urine passage of the penis (urethra), rectum, and the throat. A urine test, amplified CT, is very sensitive to detect chlamydia infection. It is convenient for testing males and females especially the females who have recently done their Pap smear within the last couple of months.

[B] Treatment

How is chlamydia treated?

Medications for treating chlamydia are azithromycin 1gm once by mouth or doxycycline 100 mg twice daily by mouth for 7 days. Other medications are erythromycin, ofloxacin, and amoxicillin. Doxycycline and ofloxacin should not be given to a pregnant patient.

[B] Pelvic inflammatory disease (PID) and infertility

What happens when someone gets pelvic inflammatory disease (PID) because of chlamydia and or gonorrhea infection?

PID is the spread of chlamydia and gonorrhea infection to the uterus (endometritis), the fallopian tube (salpingitis), the ovary (oophoritis), and to other pelvic structures. The symptoms and signs are lower abdominal pain, fever, pain in the vagina and pelvis on having sex (dyspareunia), vaginal discharge, and pain on touching and moving the cervix. It is treated with doxycycline 100mg twice daily and cefotetan 2g intravenously every twelve hours in the hospital for a very sick patient or outpatient treatment with ceftriaxone 250mg injection once and then doxycycline 100mg twice daily for ten to fourteen days.

PID may lead to a collection of inflammatory fluid in the fallopian tube and the ovary (tubo-ovarian abscess), scarring and blockage of the fallopian tubes, ectopic pregnancy, adhesion of pelvic structures, chronic pelvic pain, and infertility. In extreme cases the adhesions bind the pelvic structures together to form a frozen pelvis. The chance of infertility is 15 percent after first episode of PID, 25 percent after two episodes, and 60 percent after three episodes. Completion of treatment and cure for chlamydia and gonorrhea is very important and must be taken seriously to prevent PID and infertility.

When a female is diagnosed with PID, it is advisable to discuss concerns of her ability and chances to become pregnant with a doctor who makes the diagnosis and treat pelvic inflammatory disease.

Syphilis

Syphilis is a sexually transmitted disease caused by a type of bacteria known as a spirochete. The specific spirochete that causes syphilis is *Treponema pallidum.*

[**Figure 3a: The bacteria that causes syphilis**]

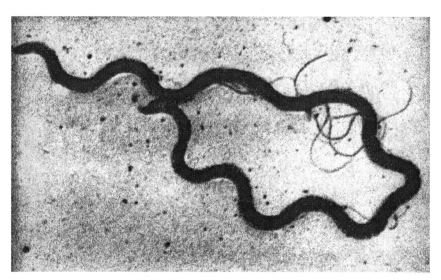

How can I get syphilis?

People get syphilis by having any kind of sex with someone who has the sore of syphilis (it is called a chancre) or the very small swellings (condylomata lata) associated with syphilis infection. A pregnant woman can pass the infection to the unborn baby if she is not treated.

[B] Stages of syphilis

What happens when someone gets syphilis?

Syphilis infection begins to show up at the site of sexual contact, and the first stage of syphilis is known as primary syphilis. This shows up within ten to ninety days after having syphilis infection as a sore that does not hurt (a painless sore) called soft chancre at any of these parts of the body: on or under the penis, on the vagina or the cervix, the anus or rectum ("butt"), and the mouth or throat where these parts of the body came into contact with the sore of someone who has syphilis.

Because the sore is painless, people may ignore it or will not even see it. It will heal within three to six weeks even without medical treatment, but that does not mean that the disease is cured. In case it is not treated, no symptoms and signs of syphilis may be seen for the next four to ten weeks after the sore disappears. This stage is called early latent syphilis.

[Figures 3b, 3c: Syphilis sore on penis; syphilis sore on the vagina]

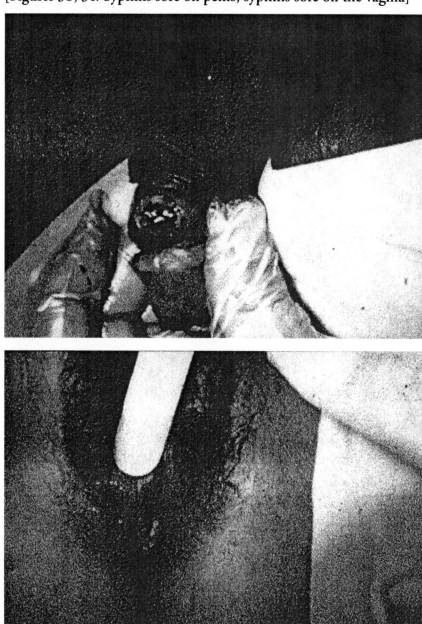

A person who has early latent syphilis is less likely to pass the infection to the sex partner because there is no sore, but the person is not cured. If a person who has early latent syphilis is not treated, the disease develops to the next stage called secondary syphilis.

A person who has secondary syphilis develops swelling of the glands draining fluids into blood (these are the lymph nodes) in the groin and a rash on the trunk of the body or all over the body, the palms and soles of the feet (palmer and plantar rash), and small swellings like warts called condylomata lata. The condylomata lata may be seen on the vagina, cervix, and throat or in the anus and rectum. The rash of secondary syphilis disappears within two to six weeks, but it may take up to three months to disappear even if no medications are taken.

[Figures 3d, 3e, 3f: Rash on the trunk of the body; rash on the hands; small wart-like swelling (condylomata lata) on the vagina]

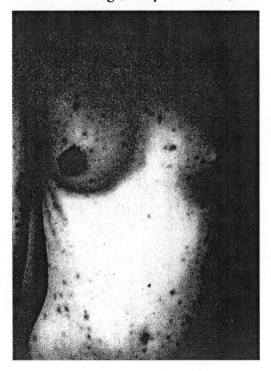

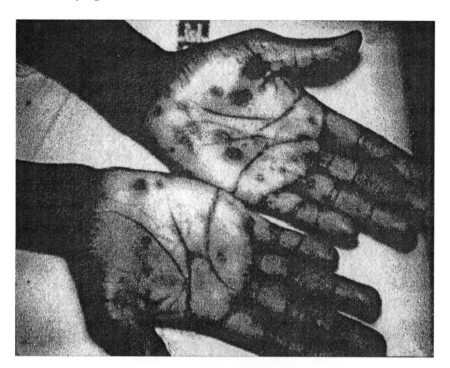

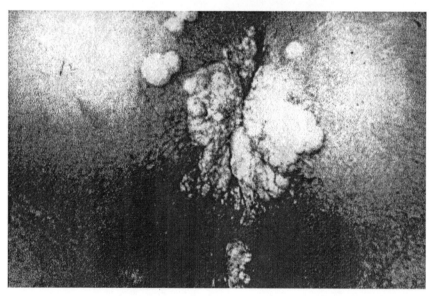

After the secondary stage of syphilis, a person with syphilis will not show any signs and symptoms for a couple of months. When this stage occurs within a year, it is called early latent syphilis. Note that early latent syphilis occurs between primary and secondary syphilis and between the end of secondary syphilis and late stage of syphilis. The stage of syphilis after one year is called late stage of syphilis.

The late stage of syphilis is divided into a late latent syphilis and a tertiary syphilis. After one year of syphilis, a person is said to have late latent syphilis if there are no symptoms and signs at all. Tertially syphilis occurs after a year of syphilis infection when syphilis infection spreads to the brain, spinal cord, and blood vessels, especially to the biggest blood vessel in the body called the aorta, and to bones and other organs in the body.

The spread of syphilis infection to the brain is known as neurosyphilis. It presents as confusion, impaired consciousness, and dysfunction of nerves in the head, face, and neck called meningoencephilitis, loss of memory (dementia), localized swelling of parts of the brain (gumma), loss of ability of the eye to accommodate light vision (Argyll Robertson pupils), and loss of sensation, balance, and tapping gait (tabes dorsalis). A spread of syphilis to the aorta leads to inflammation, swelling, and enlargement of parts of the aorta called an aneurysm, which can burst (dissecting aneurysm) leading to profuse internal bleeding and death. A localized swelling of part of the heart (aneurysm) can occur. Syphilis may be seen in the skin as localized swelling (gumma).

It is important to note that complications of syphilis, especially the infection of the brain such as meningoencephilitis, is more common in patients who have HIV/AIDS, and the signs and symptoms may be seen as part of early stages of syphilis. The staging of syphilis is important because the treatment of the stages is different.

[B] Congenital syphilis

When a pregnant woman gets syphilis and she is not treated, the baby may develop body abnormalities of the heart, brain, bones, teeth (Hutchison teeth), the head and face especially the nose and the upper airway structures. The abnormalities can occur before birth (congenital diseases), and the baby may die before or soon after birth. Therefore it is important that all pregnant women should be screened for syphilis at the first prenatal visit to the clinic or hospital. Pregnant women who have multiple sex partners and lifestyle choices such as drug abuse should repeat the test for syphilis at twenty-eight to thirty-two weeks and at delivery. In case of a stillbirth after twenty weeks, a syphilis test should be done.

In case a pregnant woman has syphilis, an ultrasound examination of the baby should be done by the twentieth to fortieth weeks of pregnancy to make sure that the baby has no body abnormalities. The ultrasound may help to rule out obvious congenital abnormalities.

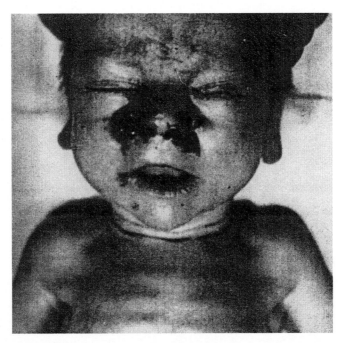

[Figure 3g, 3h: A baby with complications from syphilis infection (congenital syphilis)]

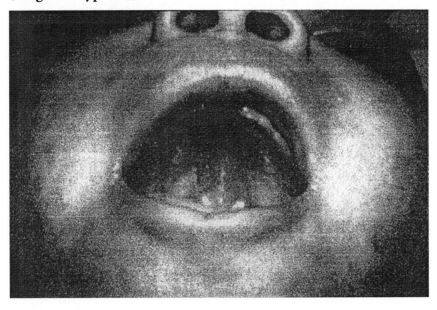

B] Diagnosis and treatment

What tests can I do to find out if I have syphilis?

The following tests can be done to diagnose syphilis.

1. The scrapings of the sore of primary syphilis can be examined under microscope by darkfield exam or immunofluorescence to find the *Treponema pallidum* that cause syphilis. The sore does not hurt, so there is no pain when the doctor is scraping it for a sample to diagnose syphilis.

2. Blood screening test for non-specific syphilis antigens called rapid plasma reagin (RPR) or Venereal Disease Research Laboratory (VDRL) is used to find the levels of the syphilis in the body. When RPR is positive and the level is 1:4 or more, it may imply that a person has been exposed to syphilis. Either of the confirmation tests of the blood for specific syphilis antigen by immunoflorescence test known as fluorescent treponemal antibody-absorbed (FTA-ABS), enzyme-linked immunoassay (IgG EIA) for the specific syphilis antigens test or microhemagglutination assay for *Treponema pallidum* (MHA-TP) is done for diagnosis.

3. In case a spread of syphilis to the brain is suspected by the doctor especially in patients with immunodeficiency such as HIV/AIDS, a VDRL test of the fluid in the brain known as cerebrospinal fluid (csf), which continues to flow through the spinal cord, is done under localized anesthesia at the back of the body in between the back bones, to make

sure that syphilis has not spread to the brain. This is very important because the treatment is intravenous penicillin, which is different from the treatment of other stages of syphilis. The test of csf for syphilis will help to prevent the development of complications of the syphilis infection of the brain that cannot be reversed. Discuss the details of testing of syphilis with your doctor.

How is syphilis treated?

1. The treatment for primary, secondary, and early latent syphilis (syphilis within a year) is Benzathine Penicillin G 2.4 mu* injection as a single dose (mu means million units). The other medications that can be used are doxycycline 100mg by mouth twice daily for two weeks, tetracycline, or ceftriaxone

2. Treatment for late latent syphilis (that is, syphilis has been present for more than one year) is Benzathine Penicillin G 2.4 mu injection once every week for three weeks, a total of 7.2 mu.

3. Syphilis in the brain (neurosyphilis) is treated with aqueous crystalline penicillin G 3 to 4 mu intravenously every four hours for ten to fourteen days. A combined treatment of procaine penicillin and probenecid can be used.

A person diagnosed with syphilis is encouraged to discuss the details of treatment with the doctor and make sure that the treatment is complete. The RPR will continue to be positive but the level will be low (e.g., RPR 1:1) after a cure and the FTA-ABS will always be positive, but it does not mean that the person still has syphilis. In case a person has new or early syphilis, the RPR is usually greater than 1:4

It is important that a pregnant woman who has syphilis and has allergy to penicillin is made less allergic by desensitization to penicillin by an allergy doctor and then treated with penicillin to ensure a cure for syphilis and to prevent the baby from getting syphilis infection. Follow up testing with RPR levels is necessary at six weeks, three months, and six months from the time of first treatment, and the baby must be screened to make sure that the baby has no syphilis infection. Treatment of a baby who is exposed to syphilis or tests positive for syphilis is beyond the scope of this book, and a consultation with a doctor is necessary.

How can I make sure that my sex partner is completely treated?

Treatment is given to sex partners of people diagnosed with primary, secondary, and early latent syphilis, especially sex partners within the last ninety days. The long-term partners of patients with late latent syphilis may be tested and treated based on the test results.

The sex partners most likely to have been exposed to active infectious syphilis and need to be treated to prevent the spread of syphilis are

1. A sex partner within three months plus the number of weeks of symptoms and sore for primary syphilis

2. Sex partners for the past six months plus the number of weeks of symptoms of rash in the palms and soles of the feet

(i.e., palmar and plantar rash) or body rash for secondary syphilis

3. Sex partners within the past year to the date of the diagnosis of early latent syphilis

In general, all sex partners within the last year to the time of diagnosis and the last sex partner will benefit from testing, treatment, and prevention of spread of syphilis to other sex partners. Health workers do not want the unborn child to die from syphilis or to develop congenital diseases. Therefore all sex partners need to be confidentially informed, tested, and treated.

Chancroid

Hemophilus ducreyi is the bacteria that cause chancroid.

How can I get it?

A person can get chancroid by having sex with someone who has it.

[B] Symptoms and signs

What happens when someone gets chancroid?

When a person gets chancroid, it can spread from the skin to the lymph nodes in the groin and then into the blood. It takes about ten to fourteen days to show signs and symptoms of painful ulcers on the genitals and painful swellings of the glands (bubo) in the groin. The swollen glands in the groin may have discharge oozing from them.

A high chance of HIV infection has been found among people who get chancroid, syphilis, and genital herpes because all three of them cause ulcers on the genitals and make it easier for HIV to get into the blood of a person. Therefore all sex partners of a person who has any of these diseases need to be examined and tested for HIV. A complication of chancroid is scarring of the glands in the groin (inguinal lymph nodes).

[B] Diagnosis and treatment

In case a person has a genital ulcer, what can the person do to make sure it is not chancroid?

A swab of the ulcer is sent to the laboratory for culture to detect the bacteria known as *Hemophilus ducreyi.*

How is chancroid treated?

The medications used to treat chancriod are azithromycin 1gm single dose to be taken by mouth. Chancroid can be cured. Other medications used are ceftriaxone or ciprofloxacin. Treatment of sex partners within the ten days prior to the beginning of the symptoms is recommended.

Granuloma inguinale (donovanosis):

Bacteria called *klebsiella granulomatis* cause granuloma inguinale. It is rare in the United States, but is common in India, Papua New Guinea, Central Australia, and South Africa.

How can someone get donovanosis?

People get donovanosis by having sex with someone who has it

[B] Symptoms and signs

What happens after you get it?

The bacteria will cause a painless red ulcer on the genitals. The ulcer has more blood vessels in it and can bleed if touched.

[B] Diagnosis and Treatment

How can donovanosis be diagnosed?

Donovanosis can be diagnosed by looking at the scraping (a piece of tissue, called a biopsy) of the ulcer under the microscope. Dark staining donovan bodies are seen.

What medications are used to treat donovanosis?

Doxycycline is the antibiotic used to treat it for three weeks and can be continued until all the ulcers are healed. The ulcer can come back if the treatment is not complete. Gentamycin is used to treat the ulcer that is not healing. The other antibiotics that can be used for treatment are azithromycin, ciprofloxacin, bactrim, and erythromycin.

Lymphogranuloma venerum (LGV)

Lymphogranuloma venerum (LGV) is caused by another type of chlamydia trichomatis. These types are called L1, L2, and L3.

How can someone get LGV?

A person can get LGV by having sex with someone who has it.

[B] Symptoms and signs

What happens when you get it?

It takes about two months after sexual contact for this disease to show up. The bacteria spread into the lymph nodes in the groin, and these glands swell up. These big swollen glands are called bubo, and they are painful. They are usually found in the left or the right side of the groin. The bubo can be seen on the genitalia. They burst and ooze a discharge and become a painful ulcer. Complications noted in those who have sex in the butt are pain on passing stool, holes between the skin of the anus and the rectum (called a fistula), and narrowing (stricture) of the rectum.

[B] Diagnosis and treatment

How is it diagnosed?

A swab of the discharge is sent to the laboratory for culture and identification. Other lab tests for chlamydia can be done when the doctor finds them to be helpful for diagnosis.

What is the treatment for LGV?

Doxycycline is taken for twenty-one days for a cure. Erythromycin can also be used to treat it.

Hepatitis B infection

Hepatitis means inflammation of the liver. Hepatitis B infection is caused by a virus called hepatitis B virus (HBV).

[B] Transmission

How can you get hepatitis B infection?

Hepatitis B virus is found in the semen of the sperm, vaginal secretions, blood, saliva, wound discharges, and other body fluids of someone who has hepatitis B.

People can get hepatitis B virus into their body by doing any of the following:

Having sex with someone who has it, sharing of needles to inject drugs, sharing of razors, transferring from mother to child at birth and breastfeeding, getting a blood transfusion of blood that has hepatitis B virus, and having a needle stick injury during intravenous or surgical procedure on a person who has hepatitis B virus.

[B] Symptoms and signs

What happens when you get hepatitis B virus infection?

It takes six weeks to six months for the hepatitis B virus to start causing changes in the body and show symptoms and signs. About half of the people who get it will not show any signs or symptoms at all. One person out of hundred (1 percent) will have severe (acute) liver failure and death within a short time of infection. Infants and children who are younger than five years usually acquire the disease from a mother with hepatitis B virus and suffer severely and will have disease for a long time (chronic infection). About two to six out of a hundred adults will have chronic hepatitis, and about a quarter (25 percent) of such persons will die early from incurable, deadly end stage inflammation of the liver called cirrhosis or liver cancer (hepatocellular carcinoma) (*MMWR* 2006).

When hepatitis B virus gets into the body, it will lodge in the liver and multiply. The usual initial signs are fever and jaundice. The symptoms are nausea and vomiting and abdominal pains. When the treatment is not done early or when the body's immune system is not able to overcome the infection, then the infection will remain in the person and the person is known as a carrier of hepatitis B infection. A carrier of hepatitis B infection can pass it on to other people. Therefore, a person who is diagnosed with hepatitis B must not share needles, syringes, razors, or toothbrushes and avoid having unprotected sex and must use condoms for all sexual activities or stay abstinent from sex with other people if possible.

[B] Diagnosis

What test can I do to find out that I have hepatitis B infection?

Hepatitis B can be diagnosed by a blood test to detect a protein (antigen) produced by the virus called hepatitis B surface antigen (HBsAg) or the genes of the hepatitis B virus called HBV DNA. Anytime you do a blood test and it shows that you have HBsAg or HBV DNA, it means that you have hepatitis B infection.

The other antigens that help with the diagnosis and treatment of hepatitis B are hepatitis B core antigen (HBcAg) and Hepatitis B e antigen (HBeAg). When you have HBsAg and then HBeAg in your blood, it means you are highly infectious and can easily pass on HBV to other people.

When the body's defense system (immune system) is able to produce certain proteins known as antibodies that attack the hepatitis B virus to destroy it and make the virus harmless, the person may or not be cured from hepatitis. When the immune system produces anti-hepatitis B surface antibodies (anti-HBs) to destroy hepatitis B surface antigens (HBsAg) and clear it from the body, it means the person is cured and a follow-up test for hepatitis B will show anti-HBs, anti-hepatitis B core antibodies (anti-HBc) and no HBsAg. In case the immune system produces anti-hepatitis B e antibodies (anti-HBe) to try and destroy the hepatitis B e antigen (HBe Ag), it means the ability to pass on the infection to other people has reduced.

When you get a vaccination for hepatitis B virus and then you come into contact with hepatitis B virus from another person, your body will produce antibodies to try to destroy the hepatitis B virus. In most cases the hepatitis B virus is destroyed and you do not get the disease. When you do have a hepatitis B test, your results will show anti-HBs and anti-HBc antibodies.

In situations where a person gets hepatitis B vaccination and has not come into contact with hepatitis B virus, the test for hepatitis B virus infection will show only anti-HBs antibodies. In case someone is found to have hepatitis B virus infection and the person is not cured within six months, the person is said to have a chronic hepatitis B virus infection. And such a person is a carrier of hepatitis B virus and can pass on the disease to other people.

[B] Vaccination and active prevention

How can a person prevent coming into contact with hepatitis B?

The basic prevention measures are the same as those for all STDs. Vaccination before coming into contact with hepatitis B virus (preexposure vaccination) is recommended for all children by completion of the childhood immunization schedule, sexually active adolescents, young adults and adults who were not previously immunized, injection drug users, homosexuals, all unvaccinated persons seeking treatment for STDs, household and sexual contacts of HBsAg positive patients (because they are carriers), residents and employees of institutions for the mentally retarded, individuals who receive multiple transfusions of blood (e.g., sickle cell anemia patients) and blood products (e.g., hemophilia A and B patients) and transplant recipients, patient with chronic kidney failure and on dialysis, health care workers, travelers for more than six months to places where hepatitis B infection is high, and native Alaska and Pacific Islanders. All of these groups of people should receive a series of three vaccinations on day one, then thirty days later and six months later before they come into contact with the HBV virus. [Sickle cell anemia is an inherited disease of the red blood cells that cause change in the shape of some of the red blood cells and decrease the function to carry oxygen in the blood. Hemophilia A and B are inherited diseases causing the blood to have difficulty clotting.]

People can be vaccinated and prevented from getting HBV infection within a short time after they are aware that they have come into contact with hepatitis B virus (i.e., postexposure vaccination). For instance, when a person's sex partner is found to have hepatitis B virus (an HBsAg positive partner), that person may be protected from getting hepatitis B infection if HBV vaccine and hepatitis B immune globulin are given within two days to seven days after sexual exposure and a second vaccination thirty days later (Washington Manual of Medical Therapeutics 2001).

A baby born to a mother who tested HBsAg positive must receive hepatitis B vaccine and hepatitis B immune globulin within twelve hours of birth. A follow-up test should be done when the baby is one year old, for anti-HBc and anti-HBs antibodies to show that the baby is cured. In case the baby tests positive for HBsAg or HBV DNA, it means that the baby has hepatitis B infection. The treatment of HBV infection in children must be discussed with a doctor.

[B] Treatment

What medications are used to treat hepatitis B?

The medications used to treat hepatitis B are interferon alpha 2b, lamivudine, and adenofovir. Any of these medications can be used alone or in combination. Discuss the details of treatment of hepatitis B virus infection with your doctor. The sex partner should be referred for testing and treatment.

[B] Complications

What will eventually happen to someone who is not cured of hepatitis B?

A person who is not cured for acute hepatitis B infection will develop chronic hepatitis, which may progress to cancer of the liver (hepatocellular carcinoma) or end stage inflammation and fibrosis of the liver (cirrhosis) within twenty to thirty years from time of diagnosis. Alcohol should be avoided and a regular follow up with a doctor to screen for these two deadly complications is important for all who have chronic hepatitis B infection.

Hepatitis C infection

Hepatitis C infection is caused by the hepatitis C virus (HCV).

[B] Transmission

How can a person get hepatitis C infection?

A person can get hepatitis C by having sex with someone who has it, and a hepatitis C positive mother can pass it on in her blood to the baby at the time of birth. Most people get it by sharing needles and syringes to inject themselves with illegal drugs like heroin. It is more infectious than hepatitis B. Blood, blood products, and organs for transplant that are not screened for hepatitis C can be a source of infection at the time of blood and blood products transfusion and organ transplant.

Currently blood and blood products as well as organs for transplant are screened for both hepatitis B and C before they are used. The chances of getting both hepatitis B and hepatitis C from these sources have remarkably reduced.

When a person gets hepatitis C virus infection, it takes about two weeks to six months (known as the incubation period) before the infection is established in the body. The person will then show symptoms and signs of the disease.

[B] Symptoms and signs

How can I know that I have hepatitis C?

A person who has hepatitis C may not show any symptoms and signs at all until a test is done to detect it. Most people have nausea and vomiting and discomfort or pain in the right upper part of the belly (abdomen). When the disease progresses and the liver starts to fail, a yellow color of the eyes, palms, and soles of the feet and nails (called jaundice) and acute confusion and impairment of consciousness due to liver disease (hepatic encephalopathy) can occur. A screening and confirmation test is necessary for diagnosis.

[B] Complications

What happens when a person gets hepatitis C infection?

When hepatitis C virus gets into the body, it affects mostly the liver. It causes infection and inflammation of the liver. There is an 80 percent chance that the infection will continue for more than six months to several years and become a chronic inflammation of the liver (chronic hepatitis). Complications of this disease are early death from acute hepatitis C and hepatic encephalopathy, end stage inflammatory liver disease (cirrhosis), and cancer of the liver (hepatocellular carcinoma) also known as hepatoma. These deadly complications eventually occur within twenty to thirty years from the time of infection.

[B] Diagnosis

What test can I do to find out if I have hepatitis C?

Hepatitis C is screened by a blood test for antibodies produced by the body's defense system to fight and kill the hepatitis C virus called anti-hepatitis C antibodies (anti-HCV). When you have anti-HCV in your blood, it means you have come into contact with hepatitis C, and the gene for hepatitis C virus (HCV RNA) is checked to confirm the infection. The HCV RNA can be detected in the blood within one to three weeks after coming into contact with it by a test called polymerase chain reaction (PCR). The anti-HCV can be detected in the blood by two weeks to six months.

All blood and blood products and organs for transplant are tested for hepatitis C, so it is less likely for someone to get hepatitis C virus with this modern medical practice from screened blood, blood products, and organs for transplant.

[B] Prevention and treatment

How can I prevent hepatitis C infection?

The prevention of hepatitis C is the same as the prevention for hepatitis B and other STDs. The most important preventive measures are the screening of blood and blood products and no sharing of needles and syringes. Those who inject drugs like heroin have a higher risk of getting hepatitis C infection and should not share needles and syringes. Remember that there is no vaccine available to protect us from hepatitis C. Therefore, it is important to do everything possible to prevent this deadly infection.

What is the treatment for hepatitis C?

The medications used are ribavirin and pegylated interferon. Consult your doctor for details of treatment and continue the follow up of the liver function test. Most people are not cured of hepatitis C virus that eventually leads to cirrhosis of the liver or cancer of the liver. Drinking alcohol worsens hepatitis C and its complications. Any person who has hepatitis B and C must avoid drinking alcohol.

Genital herpes

Genital herpes is caused by herpes simplex virus (HSV).

[B] Herpes simplex 1 and 2 infection

There are two types of herpes simplex virus that a person can get by having sex. These are herpes simplex 1 (HSV-1) and herpes simplex 2 (HSV-2). HSV-2 is the most common cause of recurrent genital herpes. At least fifty million people in the U.S. have genital HSV infection (*MMWR* 2006).

Remember that it is a chronic infection and has no cure. It can be kept under control by medications, but the virus remains in the nerves for life and can reappear in a form of painful rash anytime a person's immune system is weakened as in the case of HIV/AIDS.

Also weakened are people on cancer treatment and those who receive transplants and take medications that suppress the immune systems. Herpes can reappear in cases of other serious diseases or illness.

How can I get genital herpes?

You can get genital herpes by having sex with someone who has it. Many people who have HSV-2 do not show any rash on their genitals (such as on the penis or vagina) but will have the virus on the inside of the genitals and pass it on to their sex partner through sexual intercourse or by deep kissing with exchange of saliva which contains HSV, most commonly HSV-1, with their sex partner.

[B] Symptoms and signs

What happens when a person gets genital herpes?

Within a few days to weeks of coming into contact with HSV, a person develops multiple groups of painful rashes, which contain fluid (blisters). These blisters burst and become painful ulcers. HSV then spreads into the nerves especially the nerves (posterior ganglion of the nerve) in the genital area. Other symptoms noted are swelling of the lymph nodes in the groin, muscle pain (myalgia), fever and headache especially when the HSV spreads to the membrane that covers the brain (i.e., aseptic meningitis). HSV especially HSV-1 can also spread to the brain and cause acute confusion and seizures, a complication known as herpes encephalitis.

The HSV hiding in the nerves can reappear anytime the immune status is weak and the painful rash is noted. It could be a marker that a person who has HIV infection has progressed to AIDS.

A pregnant woman can pass on the infection to the baby in the womb, and the baby will develop congenital diseases. It is important to note that when a pregnant woman has active herpes simplex rash on the genitals, it is recommended that she deliver the baby by caesarian section (surgery to remove the baby) to avoid passing on the virus to the baby.

[B] Diagnosis

What test is done to find out if someone has genital herpes?

Scrapings from the bottom of the ulcer and the rash are taken and examined under the microscope. This test is known as Tzanck preparation. Cultures and PCR testing for the HSV DNA can be done to find HSV in the fluid of the brain (cerebrospinal fluid) collected from the spinal cord by spinal tap when the spread of the virus to the brain is suspected especially in AIDS patients.

[B] Treatment

What medications are used to treat genital herpes?

The following medications are used: acyclovir, valacyclovir and famciclovir. Treatment may reduce the rate of recurring painful rash by 70 to 80 percent, which is beneficial when a person has frequent breakouts six or more times in a year. Treatment reduces the chance of passing HSV-2 to a sex partner (Romanowski 2003).

Genital warts (condylomata acuminata)

Genital warts are caused by the human papilloma virus (HPV).

[B] Types of human papilloma virus (HPV) and cervical cancer

There are many types of HPV. The HPV types 6 and 11 are the common causes of genital warts. HPV types 16, 18, 31, 33, and 35 can cause cervical cancer. HPV types 16 and 18 are the most common causes of cervical cancer. The availability of a vaccine called Gardasil for prevention of HPV and frequent Pap smears will help to reduce and check for cervical cancer.

[Figure 10a: Genital warts on the vagina caused by human papilloma virus]

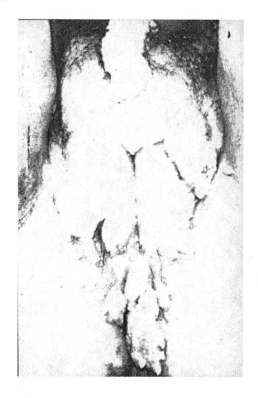

How can I get HPV?

A person can get HPV by having sexual contact with someone who has genital warts. It is highly infectious even on casual contact on the genitals.

[B] Symptoms and signs

What happens when someone comes into contact with HPV?

The HPV infection takes a varied period of time to show up. The infection can be cleared by the body's immune system, but most cases are not cleared and show up as swellings (tags) of skin called genital warts. Note that genital warts can be flat and not easily found until a test is done. It may not show any symptoms at all but can be itchy and painful and pieces of it can easily break off (friable). These genital warts are usually found on the urethra, vulva, and vagina, cervix, scrotum, penis, anus and rectum ("butt"). Genital warts have also been found in the mouth, the throat, the nose, and the conjunctiva of the eye in those who perform oral sex.

[Figure 10b: Genital warts on the penis caused by human papilloma virus]

The fact that HPV types 16, 18, 31, 33, and 35 can cause cancer of the cervix, vulva, penis, the anus and rectum, and the throat is very important. When a Pap smear is found to be abnormal, it is advisable to do a test (HPV DNA) for HPV especially for the types 16 and 18

since HPV increases the chance that the woman may have cervical cancer in the future.

[B] Diagnosis

What can be done to find out if I have HPV?

The tests used to diagnose HPV are the direct examination of the visible genital warts and biopsy, Pap smear, HPV DNA, and examination of the cervix with acetic acid for flat genital warts.

[B] Treatment and prevention

Can genital warts be cured?

Treatment depends on the size, number of warts, and parts of the body affected. Treatment options must be discussed with the doctor. Genital warts can be removed but can come back, and the removal of warts does not reduce the chance of passing the infection to the sex partner. Most genital warts respond to these types of treatment within three months.

1. Podofilox 0.5% solution applied twice a day for three days when the part of the body affected is up to 10cm by 10cm. Do not use more than 0.5ml per day. There is no treatment for the next four days. Treatment is continued for four weeks.

2. Imiquimod 5% cream is applied once daily at bedtime every

other day for four months. The cream is washed off six to ten hours after it has been applied to the genital warts.

3. Cryotherapy using liquid nitrogen can be done by a doctor once a week or once every two weeks. This treatment will destroy the warts. It is the treatment of choice recommended for vaginal, urethral, and anal warts.

4. Podophyllin resin 10% –25% can be applied once a week to each wart and allowed to air dry. The doctor applies it. Less than 0.5ml is applied to a part of the body with lesions less than 10cm by 10cm, but it is not applied to open sores of the warts. Wash it off one to four hours as a precaution to prevent side effects of the medication especially to prevent irritation and absorption of podophyllin into the blood.

5. Trichloroacetic acid (TCA) or Bichloroacetic acid (BCA) 80%–90%. A small amount is applied only to the wart by the doctor and allowed to dry.

A person can apply podofilox 0.5% and imiquimod 5% cream as directed by the doctor. The doctor does cryotherapy, podophyllin resin and TCA or BCA treatment. Doctors can also do surgery such as excision, curettage, electrocautery, and carbon dioxide laser surgery to remove a large number of genital warts.

6. Interferon can be injected into the warts (i.e., intralesional interferon). The side effect is pain and burning at the injection site, but it is a very effective treatment.

Remember that imiquimod, podophyllin, and podofilox should not be used during pregnancy. A pregnant woman who has genital warts and HPV types 6 and 11 can pass the infection to the baby. The baby may develop genital warts in the larynx of the airway (causing respiratory papillomatosis). Cesarean section is done when the genital warts are blocking the vagina and when the doctor finds that there could be more bleeding if the baby is delivered through the vagina.

A pregnant woman who has genital warts can have them removed. The treatment must be discussed with the doctor before the baby is born. The obstetrics and gynecologist specialist must do treatment of genital warts on the cervix and the vagina. A Pap smear or biopsy or both are done to make sure that the woman has no cancer of the cervix. Regular and consistent Pap smears or biopsy or surgery is usually recommended to prevent cervical cancer. Consultation with a doctor for an individual treatment plan is recommended.

How can I prevent HPV?

Consistent use of condoms might reduce the chance of getting genital warts and cervical cancer, but genital warts can be seen in the parts of the genitals such as the scrotum, on top of the vagina (vulva) and the area around the anus and rectum not covered by the condom (Hogen Woning 2003).

The vaccine Gardasil prevents four types of HPV infection including types 16 and 18. It is 100 percent effective in preventing genital warts and cervical cancer when vaccination is completed before a woman comes into sexual contact with HPV. The CDC recommends the vaccination to girls and women ages nine to twenty-six. But, it is advisable to discuss the side effects with your doctor and avoid getting the vaccine if your age is not appropriate because of the side effects. It may be safer for ages from seventeen to twenty-six. Three vaccine shots are given. The second shot is given two months after the first, and the third shot is given six months later. Gardasil is not recommended for pregnant women and men until further studies are completed.

Approximately 6.2 million new HPV infections occur in the U.S. every year. HPV vaccination has been found to be effective and can prevent most of these millions of infections. It is highly recommended to discuss with the doctor about vaccination and side effects.

Trichomoniasis ("Tric")

Trichomoniasis is caused by a parasitic worm (a protozoa) called *trichomonas vaginalis*. It has flagella and can move. It is commonly called "tric" in the community.

How can I get trichomoniasis?

A person can get it by having sex with someone who has it.

[B] Symptoms and signs

What happens after you get it?

Within five to seven days after having sex with someone who

has "tric," a woman may have a bad smelling, frothy, yellowish-green vaginal discharge and itching, pain on having sex, inflammation of the cervix (strawberry cervix), and redness of the vulva or the vagina. Most women and men who have "tric"do not show any symptoms at all (i.e. asymptomatic infection).

[B] Diagnosis

What test is done to diagnose "tric?"

Some of the discharge is prepared by addition of saline and examined under a microscope (i.e. wet mount) to find the mobile worm, *trichomonas vaginalis.* If there is no obvious discharge, a swab of the urethra in men and cervix of the vagina can be done and sent to the laboratory for culture to diagnose "tric."

[B] Treatment

What medication is used to treat "tric"?

Metronidazole (flagyl) 2gm to be taken once by mouth is the treatment of choice. Tinidazole can also be used.

When a pregnant woman has "tric," she needs to discuss treatment with the doctor. Note that "tric" can cause the delivery of the baby before the due date for delivery, premature rupture of the membrane that covers the baby in the womb, and low birth weight. The sex partner must be treated for "tric" to prevent getting the infection again (re-infection).

Pediculosis publis ("crabs")

Pediculosis pubis is the cause of pubic lice or "crabs" in the groin. It is a parasite that feeds on the skin.

[**Figure 12a: Crabs**]

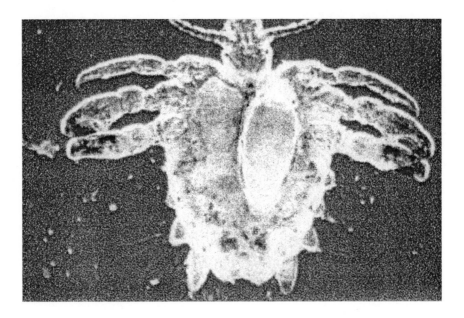

[B] Transmission

How can I get crabs?

The crabs live in the pubic hair. A person gets crabs when there is contact with a sex partner who has them in the groin (pubic area) at a time of having sex.

What happens when someone gets it?

The crab feeds on the skin and lays eggs and hatches into more crabs. It causes itching in the groin. These crabs and their eggs can be found on examination of the groin and the pubic hair.

[B] Treatment

What is the treatment for crabs?

Permethrin 1% cream is applied to the affected area in the groin and washed off after ten minutes. The other medications used to treat crabs are pyrethrins with piperonyl butoxide, malathion, and ivermectin. Contact your doctor for treatment. A person who has it and the sex partner within the previous month should be treated. All bedding and clothing should be washed to prevent getting crabs again.

Scabies

It presents as an itchy rash in the groin and sometimes between the webs of the fingers. The organism that causes it, is a skin parasite called *sarcoptes scabiei.*

[Figure 13a: Scabies mite]

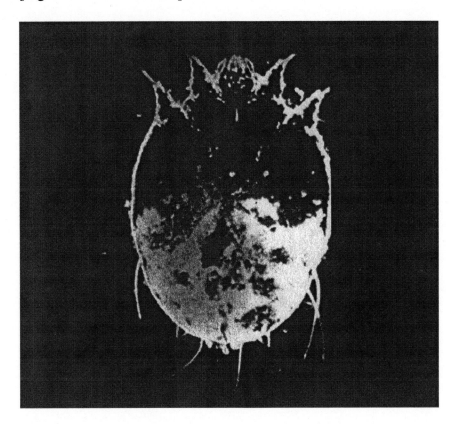

How can you get it?

You can get it by having sex with a person who has it in the groin. When you scratch the rash and the skin in the affected area of the groin, you may get the eggs under your fingernails and on your hands.

[B] Diagnosis

How can I know that the rash in my groin and hands is scabies?

The rash is very itchy and crusting and the classic finding in the web of the fingers helps to confirm it. A magnifying glass or microscope can be used to look for the parasite in the skin scrapings from the affected area. The extensive crusted rash of scabies can be found on people who have HIV/AIDS.

[B] Treatment and prevention

How is scabies treated?

Permethrin 5% cream is applied to all parts of the body from the neck down to the feet and washed off after eight to fourteen hours. The rash may not clear completely for up to fourteen days after treatment. Other medications that can be used to treat scabies are ivermectin and lindane 1%. Lindane cannot be used to treat pregnant and breastfeeding women. Contact your doctor for treatment. All bedding and clothing should be washed to avoid getting the infection back.

How can I prevent scabies?

Both sex partners and all close personal or household contacts a month before the symptoms and signs of scabies should be examined and treated.

Human immunodeficiency virus (HIV) and acquired immunodeficiency syndrome (AIDS)

HIV/AIDS is a serious STD and continues to infect and kill millions of people all around the world every year. The impact of this disease on men who have sex with men, blacks of African descent, and people of Africa and developing countries is devastating. Political will and individual sex life modification are necessary to slow down the epidemic and silence the suffering and death due to HIV/AIDS. Since the first case of HIV/AIDS was diagnosed in 1981, approximately 30 million people infected from all over the world have died.

What is worrisome about HIV infection is that new infection rates are increasing in adolescent girls and boys and young adults age fifteen to twenty-four. Some of the adolescents and young adults got the HIV infection at the time of their first sexual relationship with someone who has HIV infection. Many children are now orphans as both parents die of complications of HIV/AIDS. Although there are medications that can be given to a pregnant HIV positive woman to prevent the baby from getting the infection at the time of delivery, some pregnant women do not check for HIV infection and pass on the infection to the baby (known as vertical transmission of HIV).

Vertical transmission of HIV from pregnant mother to child can occur by transfer in the blood at the time of birth and in breast milk during breastfeeding. It is a major problem in Africa and developing countries since many HIV positive mothers cannot afford HAART and milk formula feeding and continue breastfeeding of babies even when they know that they are HIV positive.

HIV/AIDS infection

HIV infection is caused by a virus, a type of RNA virus, which changes its structure to DNA virus (that is, a retrovirus) when it enters the human body to enable it to use the proteins and nutrients in the human body cells to form billions of more HIV virus cells. The virus continues to multiply and eventually overwhelms the body's immune system in its ability to destroy or kill it from the body. [RNA virus is a virus that has a genetic makeup of ribonucleic acid]. [DNA virus, on the other hand, has a genetic makeup of deoxyribonucleic acid].

HIV infection has no cure. The multiplication of the virus within the human body can be controlled by a combination of medications known as highly active antiretroviral therapy (HAART). When a person has HIV infection and does not take medications to suppress the virus, the disease will progress to AIDS, and the person will die from the complications of AIDS.

AIDS is caused by HIV infection. The disease AIDS was first diagnosed in 1981 when previously healthy homosexual men in New York and Los Angeles were found to have pneumonia caused by the opportunistic infection called *pneumocystis carinii* (now renamed *pneumocystis jiroveci*) pneumonia and also a skin tumor called Kaposi's sarcoma. Since then the disease was seen more in homosexual men and then in those who injected drugs, or who got blood transfusions and hemophiliacs in the early 1980s (Braunwald 2001). This pattern of HIV/AIDS continued to spread among homosexuals, and for the past ten to fifteen years, more heterosexual males and females especially heterosexual black African American females have gotten HIV infection.

What is AIDS?

A person is said to have AIDS when HIV infection has progressed to suppress the person's body defense system (immune system) to the extent that the number of one of the blood cells for fighting infection—T cell lymphocytes—is reduced to below 14 percent or the lymphocytes that have a marker called CD4 (CD4 lymphocytes) count is less than 200/ul or recurrent pneumonia, cancer of the cervix, opportunistic infections such as pneumocyctis carinii pneumonia (PCP), Shingles (herpes zoster) and tuberculosis infection of the lungs.

The person gets opportunistic infections. This means that the person easily gets infected by bacteria, viruses, fungi, and parasites that are not commonly seen in healthy individuals whose immune systems are not suppressed and don't have HIV infections. Examples of opportunistic infections seen are shingles (herpes zoster), pneumocyctis carinii pneumonia (PCP), candida infection of the vagina, mouth, and the esophagus, which makes swallowing painful and difficult, and then tuberculosis (TB). Examples of the cancers noted are Kaposi's sarcoma, which are mostly seen as purple skin swellings, cancer of the cervix and also the cancer of the glands that contain part of the cells of the immune systems (lymph nodes) called lymphoma.

The only way a person who has HIV can prevent the disease from progressing to AIDS is to see the doctor for frequent checks of the immune system by measuring the amount of the HIV in the body (viral load), the number of CD4 lymphocytes (CD4 count), and to start a combination of medications for treating HIV known as highly active antiretroviral therapy (HAART). HAART is started when the doctor finds out that it is time to start the medication based on the viral load, the CD4 count, and disease complications like opportunistic infections.

[B] Transmission of HIV

How can a person get HIV?

A person can get HIV/AIDS mainly by having sex (sex in the vagina, mouth, anus and rectum) with a person who has HIV infection (i.e. sexual transmission). This can be prevented by **A**bstinence, **T**est and verify for HIV before sex, **Be** faithful to commit to one sex partner in marriage (monogamy) and **C**ondom use always (the **ATBC** prevention plan). Testing together with a "would-be sex partner" for STD and HIV infection to make an informed decision about the risk of getting HIV before commitment to a sexual relationship will be helpful to avoid coming into contact with HIV infection. It is one of the most important and firm decisions to prevent HIV infection.

A mother who has HIV can pass it in her blood to the baby at the time of birth and then through breast milk (14 percent increased risk) at time of breastfeeding after birth (i.e. vertical transmission). The chance of a pregnant woman who is HIV positive to pass on the infection to the baby at the time of birth can be reduced from 15 percent to 25 percent to less than 2 percent by the use of HIV medications and obstetrics intervention. This can be achieved by treatment with zidovudine or nevirapine and elective cesarean section at thirty-eight weeks of pregnancy and avoiding breastfeeding (Public Health Service Task Force).

Blood from a person who has HIV infection can get into another person by sharing of blood-contaminated needles and syringes to inject drugs especially among IV drug users, through a transfusion of blood and blood products, and by accidental needle sticks at the time of taking care of HIV positive patient when needles used to treat HIV patients accidentally punctured the skin of the caregiver (i.e. occupational exposure). This mode of HIV infection is called parentheral transmission of HIV.

Remember that a person can get HIV infection by three ways; sexual transmission, vertical transmission and parentheral transmission. There is no evidence that a person can get HIV by kissing, shaking hands, sharing toilet and bathrooms, eating from the same bowl or plate and drinking from the same cup.

It is advisable not to share needles, syringes, razors, and any sharp objects that can be contaminated with blood of any other person. The transmission of HIV by the transfusion of blood and blood products is rare now since blood is screened for HIV.

It is important to know that STDs such as gonorrhea, chlamydia, chancroid, syphilis, and herpes simplex cause sores that make it easy for HIV to get into the blood of a sex partner and cause HIV infection. When a person has an STD and it is not treated, there is a higher chance that the person can get HIV infection by having sex with an HIV positive person.

[B] Symptoms, signs, and complications

What happens when HIV gets into the body?

It is important to understand the changes that occur in the various parts of the body after HIV infection because it helps to explain the numerous symptoms and signs noted when a person is diagnosed with HIV/AIDS.

Within three to six weeks after HIV gets into the body, it attacks the immune system, particularly all the cells that have CD4 marker (receptors) on their surface such as lymphocytes, monocytes, and macrophages in the blood. It changes its structure from RNA retrovirus to DNA virus and uses the proteins and nutrients of the body cells to multiply. Billions of HIV are formed and continue to multiply in many body cells and spread in the blood to all parts of the body. The other cells attacked by HIV are langerhans cells in the skin and glia cells of the brain.

The person has fever and headaches, feels unwell (malaise), gets a respiratory tract infection such as the common cold, sees or feels swelling of lymph nodes, has loss of appetite, (anorexia), weight loss, diarrhea, joint pains (arthralgia), muscle pains (myalgia) and skin rash. This early stage of the disease is called acute viral syndrome.

After the acute viral syndrome, a person may feel better and may not know that there is HIV infection going on, but the HIV will continue to multiply, attack, and destroy the cells of the body's defense system. Every structure and organ of the body is affected since HIV infection multiplies in the blood cells, which are carried to every part of the body. The diseases that are seen in the body systems because of HIV infection are difficult to treat, will not respond well to treatment, or will occur again (recurrent) after treatment because the body's immune system is suppressed. These diseases associated with HIV infection are described as follows.

The diseases of the respiratory system are infection of the lungs (pneumonia) by bacteria such as *streptococcus, staphylococcus,* tuberculosis, *pneumocystis jiroveci* pneumonia when the CD4 count is less than 200/ul and mycobacterium avium complex (MAC) when the CD4 count is less than 100/ul. Infection of the sinus (sinusitis) and the bronchus (bronchitis) can occur.

The diseases of the mouth and throat (oropharynx) and the intestine (gastrointestinal system) are white patches of candida infection in the mouth, tongue, throat, and the esophagus, which make it difficult to swallow and can be a sign of progression to AIDS, white patches at the sides of the tongue called hairy cell leukoplakia caused by Epstein Barr virus, a painful ulcer at the back of the tongue and the throat (aphthous ulcers), difficulty and pain swallowing due to infection of the esophagus (esophagitis) caused by candida, cytomegalovirus or herpes simplex virus. Pain in the stomach due to lymphoma and Kaposi's sarcoma may occur.

The HIV infection of the small and large intestine will cause pain in the belly (abdominal pain) and watery diarrhea as it reduces the functions of cells in the intestines to absorb nutrients of the food into the blood. The diarrhea does not respond to conventional treatment until HIV medications are taken. The diarrhea may be caused by opportunistic infection of parasites (e.g., *cryptosporidium, isospora belli* and *microsporidia*), bacteria (e.g., campylobacter, salmonella and shigella), fungi (e.g., histoplasmosis and coccidioidomycosis) and viruses such as cytomegalovirus. Ulcers may be found in and around the rectum and the anus due to herpes simplex virus.

Patients who have a history of hepatitis B and C infection of the liver will have worsening of liver function and liver failure. When the liver fails, it is difficult for the medications used to treat HIV to work since the liver loses its function of processing the medications.

The diseases of the heart and blood vessels (cardiovascular system) are the enlargements of the heart (dilated heart), fluid around the heart (pericardial effusion) because of TB, lymphoma and Kaposi's sarcoma and bacteria infection of the lining of the heart (endocarditis) especially in IV drug users.

Diseases of the kidney, the genitals, and the urinary bladder (genitourinary) are noted. Inflammation of the kidneys due to HIV infection (HIV associated nephropathy) is more common in African

Americans. The kidneys get enlarged, and there is inflammation of the smaller arteries (capillaries) of the blood vessels in the kidney, loss of proteins especially albumin in urine, and if HIV infection is not treated, a complication of end stage kidney failure occurs. If the kidney fails, it will be difficult to treat HIV infection since most of the waste product of the medications used to treat HIV must be removed (excreted) by the kidneys to pass out of the body in urine.

Diseases of the genitals and urinary tract (genitourinary diseases) are candida infection of the vagina and the vulva (vulvoviginal candidiasis), which is noted as white discharge, itching, and a rash that may extend to the thigh.

Hormones and metabolic disorders seen in HIV patients are body fat redistribution with more fat on the belly (truncal obesity), fat pad at the back of the neck, and wasting and loss of fat in the arms and the legs, face, and buttocks. Abnormal levels of fats and lipids in the blood (lipodystrophy) are noted. High levels of triglyceride, total cholesterol, high density lipoprotein (HDL), and high levels of insulin may occur. A low level of stress-related hormones (adrenal hormones) due to opportunistic infection like tuberculosis and low levels of sodium because of inappropriately high levels of a hormone called antidiuretic hormones (ADH), which tries to help the body to retain more water, is noted. Lipodystrophy is associated with lost of fat from the extremities of the musculoskeletal systems of legs and arms and deposition of fat on the trunk and upper back and the back of the neck (called a buffalo hump).

HIV patients are also known to easily get broken bones (bone fracture) when they fall down. About 50 percent of men will have low levels of male hormones (testosterone), and about 66 percent will have decreased libido, and about 33 percent will be impotent. HIV has no significant effect on the menstrual cycle except for advanced HIV infection (Braunwald 2001).

The diseases of the blood and the blood cells (called the hemato poietic system) noted in HIV patients are low levels of hemoglobin in red blood cells known as anemia, low levels of the white blood cells (also known as leukopenia) that fight infections, low levels of platelets (known as thrombocytopenia) that work by sticking together to form clots to stop bleeding. The opportunistic infections can also cause anemia, leukopenia, and thrombocytopenia.

The skin (dermatology) diseases seen in HIV infection are various kinds of rashes such as a flaking rash in the scalp around the head, eyebrows, and the face. This is called seborrheic dermatitis. Other skin rashes may be caused by a reactivation of shingles (herpes zoster), reactivation of herpes simplex virus on the genitals, on the lips and mouth, the anus and rectum (where it is called herpes proctitis), a beefy red painful rash between the buttocks, infection of the hair follicles (folliculitis), and scabies. A rash with depression at the center (molluscum contagiosum) and worsening of genital warts by HPV can occur.

The HIV infection spreads to the brain and spinal cord (i.e. central nervous system) as well. In the brain the inflammatory cells called monocytes, which are infected by HIV, release toxins called neurotoxins, which kill brain cells (neurons). The size of the brain reduces (atrophy), the constructive thinking (cognitive) ability declines from the previous level, the person has an impaired ability to concentrate, increased forgetfulness especially short-term memory, difficulty performing complex task, dementia and behavior abnormalities, apathy and lack of initiative, agitation, and mild mania.

Any one of these various combinations of diseases can occur in a patient who has HIV. Aseptic meningitis with symptoms of headache, inability to tolerate the brightness of light (photophobia), and neck pain and stiffness (meningismus) can occur.

The opportunistic infections that affect the brain as the HIV infection progresses to AIDS are parasite infections of toxoplasmosis and cryptococcus, viral infection of cytomegalovirus (CMV), herpes simplex virus (HSV), bacteria infections of TB and mycobacterium avium complex (MAC), fungi of histoplasmosis, coccidiodomycosis, and candida. The cancers of the brain noted are lymphoma, non-Hodgkin lymphoma and Kaposi's sarcoma.

The diseases mentioned here are the most common seen in people with HIV and AIDS. Many other diseases can occur.

[B] Diagnosis of HIV infection

What test can a person do to find out about HIV infection?

The diagnosis of HIV infection begins with an HIV screening test. It is recommended that all people who are being treated for STDs should be tested for HIV. Every sexually active person should be offered HIV testing once in a year and encouraged to do HIV testing with the option to "opt-out" if a person refuses the HIV test.

The test is confidential. If a person is found to be HIV positive, the doctor and then a health department disease intervention specialist will counsel the person and contact all the sex partners and offer them the chance to test for HIV and benefit from treatment and medical care before they get seriously sick or pass the HIV on to other people.

Every person's information is confidential and that helps the health care workers to concentrate on how well everyone who tests positive for HIV can be helped to get the medical, social, mental, and other important services and provide them with the best of care to reduce suffering and harm before death.

The initial screening test is an enzyme-linked immunosorbent assay (ELISA) test to detect antibodies against HIV-1 and HIV-2. The HIV-1 is common outside Africa, and HIV-2 is mainly found in Africa. Nobody understands why two similar viruses have different distribution patterns, but we understand that the virus can change its structure.

There are many screening tests for HIV such as OraQuick Advance Rapid HIV-1/2 Antibody test, Orasure, and Polymerase Chain Reaction (PCR). PCR is most accurate and can detect the HIV in blood within three to six weeks of infection. It is used to screen donated blood and blood product for HIV before they can be used for transfusion.

OraQuick is a highly sensitive test. It is 99.6% likely to find the HIV infection in those who have a sufficient amount of HIV in their blood. It's also convenient and will be discussed in more detail in this book. The OraQuick test is a finger prick test in which a drop of blood is used for the test. It takes twenty minutes to know if the results are negative or positive. This test can detect HIV infection after three months to six months of getting HIV infection. It is advisable that when a person has a negative result, the test should be done again after three to six months.

Before the second test is done, it is advised that a person abstain from sex. When the person decides to have sex before the second test, it would be good to use condoms until the second test is done so that when the second test is negative and the person has not done anything that could have led to exposure of HIV such as IV drug abuse and sharing of needles, then it is more likely that the person has no HIV infection.

Remember that it is advisable to test together with your sex partner and that you see each others' results before you start having sex since it is good to take the precaution of not having unprotected sex with an HIV positive person or someone who does not know his or her HIV test results and may pass on HIV infection to sex partners.

It is not advisable to do OraQuick or other antibody test for a person who has already been confirmed by Western Blot or PCR or HIV RNA test to have HIV infection and has been receiving medication for HIV especially in cases when people are in doubt or relocate to another city or town for insurance purpose. In case such an antibody test in a known HIV positive person does not show up to be positive (in other words, a false negative test), that person may think that there has been a cure of HIV infection when no cure has occured. In such cases, always take a sample of whole blood from the known HIV positive person for Western Blot or PCR or HIV RNA test to keep the test results consistent with the initial test and avoid confusion.

There are medications available to suppress and slow down the HIV disease process and prevent early progression to AIDS. So it is better to test and know your results and benefit from taking the medications to avoid unnecessary suffering from serious opportunistic infections that can make life difficult and miserable.

In case a person's screening test is positive, a confirmatory blood test called Western Blot is done. The rapid test is about 99.6 percent sensitive. So when a person tests positive, it is more likely to be confirmed positive by Western Blot or PCR for HIV RNA or HIV viral culture.

[B] Counseling and testing of sex partner

What can be done for people who test positive for HIV and the sex partner?

When a person tests positive for HIV infection, it is important for that person to talk to the STD prevention counselor or disease intervention specialist and a doctor to find out what can be done to provide the emotional support, medical treatment, and answers to questions the person may have about the disease even before the confirmation result is received. It is good to talk confidentially about sex partners so that as soon as the positive result is confirmed, the health care worker assigned to help and provide a linkage to a doctor can confidentially contact the sex partners to give them a chance to get tested and benefit from treatment, services, and counseling available to all HIV positive patients. All sex partners' information is kept confidential.

Remember that unless a person tests together with a would-be sex partner before they begin to have sex and see each others' results and then consistently use condoms and repeat the test three to six months after the first test to make sure that both of them have no HIV infection at the beginning of the sexual relationship and limit sex to only each other, there will be no way of knowing who had the virus first and passed it on to the other. So for an adolescent, it is safer not to start having sex until you have someone like you who is HIV negative and ready to marry.

Every person is encouraged to give sufficient information to the health care worker—usually a doctor and STD/HIV disease intervention specialist assigned by the health department to assist with treatment and confidential notification of sex partners. This will help to provide the best of care to HIV patients and slow the spread of HIV/AIDS. When a person tests HIV positive, the disease intervention specialist assigned by the health department will link the person to a doctor, social worker, or case manager and the clinic where medical care and other social services can be provided.

It is very important that HIV positive patients see a doctor and regularly follow up with the doctor's appointment so that the health status, CD4 count, and viral load can be checked. This will enable the doctor to start the medications for treating HIV at the time it is needed most and give prophylactic medication to prevent opportunistic infections.

Besides the doctor, who else needs to know about the results of the HIV positive patient?

When a person has HIV infection, it is advised that the person's doctor and dentist are made aware so that they can provide the best of care. The person is required by law to tell the sex partner about the HIV positive results so that the sex partner can make an informed decision about prevention of HIV infection and use condoms for sex or abstain from sex.

People are different in the way their bodies handle the HIV virus. Therefore, even if an HIV positive patient decides to have sex with a sex partner who is known to be HIV positive, it is advised that condoms be used for sex because the exchange of the HIV virus may lead to resistant virus, which will not respond to the medication treatment and increase the cost of treatment. The medications previously used for treatment with better results of increasing CD4 count and lowering the amount of HIV in the body (HIV viral load) may not work. HIV positive patients are encouraged to use condoms for all sexual activities.

[B] Treatment of HIV/AIDS

How is HIV/AIDS treated?

There is no cure for HIV. There is no vaccine to prevent it even after twenty-five years of medical and scientific research because the virus keeps changing its structure. Combinations of medications called highly active antiretroviral therapy (HAART) are used to treat HIV and prevent it from progressing to AIDS. An HIV positive person needs to see a doctor regularly and consistently follow treatment to enable the medications to work and to stay healthy.

A person is started on the medications when the doctor finds out that any of the following has occurred:

1. A person has AIDS (CD4 count less than 200 or absolute T cell lymphocyte count less than 14 percent or symptoms and diagnosis of the opportunistic infections of AIDS).

2. A person has no symptoms but the CD4 count is less than 500 cells/micro liter or viral load is greater than 10,000 copies/ml by branched DNA (bDNA) test or 20,000 copies/ml by polymerase chain reaction (PCR) test.

3. A person who has no symptoms and CD4 count greater than 500 cells/micro liter or viral load less than 10, 000 copies/ml by branched DNA test or 20,000 copies/ml by PCR may be considered for treatment, but most doctors have found out that it is better to wait until the CD4 count is less than 500 cells per micro liter.

Presently, when the CD4 count is 350/ul and below that level, physicians always discuss with HIV positive persons to start getting HAART which will reduce the HIV viral load to undetectable level of less than 50 copies/ml and increase the CD4 count to the acceptable level (this means CD4 count of 500/ul and above) for better health and prevent AIDS. But such an important treatment is not readily available in the developing countries especially in Africa.

Follow-up visits to the doctor are necessary for the doctor to monitor how a person's immune system is responding to the treatment by checking the CD4 count for increase (good response) or decrease (no good response) and if the HIV level in the body is reducing (good response) or increasing (no good response). Changes of medications may be needed for a response to treatment and to reduce the side effects of the medications.

A doctor may prescribe a combination of two or three of the following medications to treat HIV:

1. Nucleoside Reverse Transcriptase Inhibitors (NRTI):

Combivir (lamivudine and zidovudine), emtricitabine (FTC), lamivudine (3TC), abavir and lamivudine, zalcitabine (ddC), zidovudine (AZT, ZDV), abacavir, tenofovir and emtricitabine, didanosine, tenofovir, stavudine

2. Non-nucleoside Reverse Transcriptase Inhibitors (NNRTI):

   etravirine, delavirdine, efavirenz, nevirapine

3. Protease Inhibitors (PI):
amprenavir (APV), tipranavir (TPV), indinavir (IDV), saquinavir, lopinavir and rotinavir (LPV/RTV), fosaprenavir, ritonavir (RTV), darunavir, atazanavir (ATV), nelfinavir (NFV)

4. Multi-class combination:

   efavirenz, emtricitabine and tenofovir

5. Fusion Inhibitors:

   enfuvirtide (T-20)

6. Early Inhibitors CCR5 co-receptor antagonist:

   maraviroc

7. HIV integrase strand transfer inhibitors:

   Raltegravir

Details of treatment of HIV with HAART should be discussed with a doctor to ensure the best of care for HIV patients and compliance of treatment.

The intermediate lifetime cost for treatment of HIV in the U.S. is approximately $195,188 (Sweat 2001). Since HIV has no cure, it means that on the average, a person who is HIV positive will need to spend about $196,000 on treatment before death. This is a huge financial burden on the individuals, the family, and the government. The government finances most of the cost. It is appropriate to understand that HIV could be a financial problem for the government and significantly affect health care costs. The cost savings for intervention such as VOICES/VOCES to prevent STD is $5,544,408 per 10,000 clients who receive the intervention (Sweat 2001).

Global HIV prevention and intervention is a social, economic, and political necessity because the cost and benefit of prevention and intervention into the spread of STD/HIV is far cheaper and better options to keep the labor force of the country healthy.

It is unfortunate that a lot of people made mistakes in the past and got HIV infection. Presently, we know so much about how we can prevent HIV infection. Therefore, let us demonstrate that we love ourselves not to suffer before death, and we care so much that we do not want to burden our government and the country with such a huge financial problem associated with HIV infection. HIV prevention works. It is a better option than early lifetime suffering, financial burden of treatment, and a preventable death.

[B] Monitoring of response to HIV treatment

Why is it important that a person who has HIV know the CD4 count and viral load?

It is very important to know the CD4 count because it is a marker of when a person who has HIV infection will develop opportunistic infections. It is therefore used to monitor the likelihood that an HIV positive person will get opportunistic infection. Then a prophylactic medication is prescribed by the doctor to prevent a specific opportunistic infection.

For example, tuberculosis can occur at any level of CD4 count and especially when the HIV positive patient is not eating good food. When the CD4 count is less than 200/ul, the *pneumocystis jiroveci* pneumonia (PCP), toxoplasma infection of the brain (encephalitis), recurrent bacteria pneumonia, and candida infections of the mouth, throat, and the esophagus can occur. A doctor can give antibiotics like bactrim to the patient to prevent PCP and toxoplasma encephalitis. Mycobacterium avium complex (MAC) infection is noted when the CD4 count is less than 100/ul. The antibiotic taken to prevent MAC is azithromycin. At the CD4 count less than 50/ul, MAC and cytomegalovirus (CMV) infection occurs. A person who has AIDS usually gets prophylactic medications.

The viral load is an indicator of the amount of the HIV virus in the body. When the level is low, it means there is less virus multiplying in the body, and it is better for a healthy body. Higher viral load means more HIV virus are multiplying in the body, and the person is more likely to pass the infection to another person without protection. Therefore, at a higher HIV viral load, the doctor will discuss the need to start HAART medications to reduce the multiplication of the HIV virus in the body and prevent the suppression of the immune system by the HIV infection and keep the body healthy. The goal of treatment and monitoring is to keep the CD4 count above 500 u/l and the viral load below 10,000 and then undetectable.

Every HIV patient should aim at compliance of treatment and getting the viral load to an undetectable level of less than 50 copies/ml, which means that the level in the body is lowered to the extent that it is not measurable in blood by the available methods used to measure the viral load. This is essential to prevent AIDS and the opportunistic infections. All HIV patients are encouraged to know and follow these levels of CD4 count and viral load with the doctor, comply with the medical treatment, and openly discuss medical care and nutrition with the medical doctor at every clinic visit.

The doctors use the levels of CD4 count and the HIV viral load to decide when HIV positive patients need to start taking the combination of medications (HAART) to suppress the multiplication of HIV in the body and prevent AIDS. Doctors monitor the trend of response to the combination of the medications a patient is taking and decide when to make changes. Most importantly, the trend of CD4 counts and viral loads over a periods of months helps the doctor to make an educated decision whether a patient is doing better on the treatment plan or to discuss reasons for failure of the treatment, risk of complications, and to do further tests to find out if the patient's HIV virus is becoming resistant to the medications in situations of treatment failure.

Prevention of HIV resistance to treatment is one of the most important part of HIV treatment and monitoring. HIV resistance means treatment failure that will rapidly cause AIDS. Medications for treating HIV resistance are more expensive. HIV patients who do not comply with treatment and those who have unprotected sex with other HIV positive patients causing exchange of the virus and double or more HIV exposures are likely to develop resistant forms of HIV and die from AIDS. Therefore, every HIV patient should remember to comply with HAART treatment for HIV, remember to keep documentation of the levels of the viral loads and CD4 counts, and make sure their doctors keep them informed about the trends of the viral load and the CD4 counts so that they will know if they are doing well on treatment before they get AIDS and its complications, which can rapidly lead to unnecessary suffering and death.

[B] Origin of HIV

What is the origin of HIV?

The origin of HIV infection is not known, but scientific theories point to the possible origin from the Pan troglodytes chimpanzees in West Equatorial Africa. Simian viruses, which are genetically similar to HIV-1 virus, were found in the chimpanzees. Some of the viruses resulted from genetic recombination. Some think that hunters may have been exposed to infected blood of these chimpanzees (National Institutes of Health).

There are two types of HIV known as HIV-1 and HIV-2. The HIV-1 is divided into three subtypes referred to as M, O and N. The M subtypes are made up of similar virus strains numbered from "A to K". Over ninety eight percent (98%) of HIV-1 infections in the U.S. are caused by the virus strains B of the M subtypes. The O subtype is 55-70% similar in amino acid structure to the M subtypes. The N subtype is a new group of HIV virus. Most O and N subtypes of HIV-1 infection in U.S. were acquired in other countries. Minority of strains of HIV-1 originate in West Africa (John G. Bartlett, 2000-2001)

The HIV-2 show 40-60% similar amino acid structure as the HIV-1. It is found primarily in West Africa. HIV-2 is 5-8 fold less efficient to be transmitted than HIV-1 in the early stage of disease and it is associated with lower viral load and slower rate of CD4 reduction and progression to AIDS. (Bartlett, 2000-2001)

The reason why HIV-2 is more common in West Africa and most parts of Africa but why HIV-1 is more common in Europe and the Western part of the world is not clearly understood. There have not been any similar studies in humans to find out if similar viruses in the same types of specimens examined in the chimpanzees could have genetically changed to HIV-1 and HIV-2. It is important to remember that there are non-virulent forms of HIV, which are not yet known to be associated with serious infection like HIV-1 and HIV-2. The subtype B of group M strain of HIV form the strain of the virulent form of HIV-1 originally described among men who have sex with men (MSM) in New York by 1981 and then in Europe. This subtype is very rare in Africa. Researchers think it was carried from Africa to Haiti before spreading to the United States and onward (Sharp, 2008).

Why is it that we did not see the epidemic of HIV-1 in Africa and Haiti within the twenty to fifty years before the HIV-1 epidemic in U.S. in the 1980s? Why is it that since 1981, millions of people have HIV-1 infection and HIV-2 infection in U.S. and Africa, respectively, and there was not such a large number of HIV infections in Africa in the 1980s? Could there be the existence of a non-virulent form of subtype B of group M strain of HIV in the U.S., which turned into a virulent form of HIV-1 because of our sexual lifestyle?

Nobody knows for sure what led to the emergence of virulent subtype B of group M strain of HIV-1 among men who have sex with men, which marked the beginning of the HIV epidemic as described among MSM in New York and Los Angeles, California in 1981. Why did it take some years before heterosexual males and then females became infected with HIV-1 in the U.S.?

All these questions are important for discussion to enable us to understand that the dynamics of the emergence of the HIV epidemic is like any other new emergent infectious disease and is rooted in our behavioral lifestyle and choices. Thus, despite the fact that the HIV epidemic has been imminent since 1981, more men have HIV (approximately 75 percent of HIV cases) than women (approximately 25 percent of HIV cases) in the United States. The reverse statement is true for Africa; more women than man have HIV in Africa.

The following news articles about the origin of HIV have been added here to stimulate group discussion and scientific curiosity among students who will be interested in pursuing medical and public health careers in the future and especially for those who will be interested in the search for a vaccine for HIV. However, it is important to point out the fact that throughout human history, diseases have been linked to behaviors especially those behaviors that deviate from the normally accepted non-harmless human endeavors. And an infectious disease like HIV is no exception. It almost always has been linked to deviant behaviors. Also, organisms such as viruses and bacteria, which have been normal flora of other species of animals, can change and mutate and become virulent and dangerous once they get into the body and the bloodstream of humans.

For example, when men go deer hunting in the northeastern part of the U.S. and in Wisconsin and Minnesota, Europe, Asia and

Australia, ticks that live on the white-tailed deer may bite them. These particular ticks are infected with bacteria called *Borrelia burgdorferi,* which will then enter the blood and the entire body of the person and can cause Lyme disease, which manifests as a rash and inflammation of joints and the lining of the heart and inflammation of the brain causing encephalitis.

Many other diseases such as leptospirosis occur by coming into contact with urine or infected tissues of animals and cause jaundice, liver failure, and kidney failure. SARS, the hantavirus infection of lungs, yellow fever, and many other deadly infectious diseases are acquired by persons who engage in behaviors and endeavors that make them get exposed to virus and bacteria, which may or may not be virulent in other animals.

For instance, severe acute respiratory syndrome (SARS) is a life-threatening viral illness caused by a corona virus known as SARS-associated corona virus (SARS-CoV). It was believed to have originated in Guangdong Province in southern China and then spread to other parts of the world in 2002. By July 2003, 8,437 people worldwide became ill with SARS and 813 died. The lifestyle of the first few people who had it were tracked to the source of infection, civet cats. Six civet cats from a restaurant where a female worker had SARS were found to have corona virus with a genetic profile similar to that of humans who had SARS.

Researchers from the World health Organization (WHO) found the virus in cages in the restaurant where a patient who had SARS ate civet meat. This virus spread from civet cat to humans. Tracking the lifestyle of people who are infected with virulent forms of virus and bacteria that cause an infectious disease epidemic may help to find the origin of a virulent forms of infection faster than tracking from nonvirulent forms.

Nonvirulent forms of HIV infection might have existed long ago and were not killing people; otherwise, it would have been described in medical literature as a killer disease as were other deadly diseases such as typhus fever, cholera, and tuberculosis, which have existed for centuries and killed people from different parts of the world. Since HIV was described in 1981, millions of people have died within the past twenty-seven years. No such epidemics associated with HIV infection were known prior to 1981. The virulent form of HIV infection may be a new disease that emerged from nonvirulent HIV as a result of our sexual and other behavioral lifestyles.

In case such virulent forms of HIV had existed for hundreds of years with the kind of urbanization and traveling that have occurred in Africa and all parts of the world even for the past fifty years, we should have expected that the numerous blood transfusions—without screening for HIV until the 1980s especially in Africa where blood transfusion in pregnant patients is common at the time of child birth and for treating childhood anemia such as sickle cell anemia—to have caused major epidemics of symptoms of HIV/AIDS and death from HIV infection before it was described in the medical literature in 1981. We have no evidence that high number of people got HIV infection from blood transfusion compare to sexual transmission in Africa.

The colonial rulers in Africa especially West Africa had very well trained physicians from Great Britain and did send local indigenous people, though few of them, for medical training in Edinburgh, Oxford, and Cambridge universities. They described many infectious diseases like yellow fever, measles, Epstein Barr virus associated lymphoma (Burkitt's lymphoma), guinea worm, and many other infections in West

Africa. At least, those physicians would have described the symptoms and signs associated with HIV/AIDS, as we know at this present time. They did not.

The French-speaking countries in central Africa had physicians trained in France and other European countries and described emergence of deadly infectious diseases like Ebola Virus. They could have at least described the symptoms and signs of virulent forms of HIV before 1981 in case such virulent forms of HIV had existed many years before 1981. They saw none. In case there had been evidence of such virulent forms of HIV in Africa before 1981 and had killed people, there would have been investigations initiated by world renowned infectious diseases consultants working in Africa for well respected organizations like WHO and CDC.

For instance, it is interesting to note that the first case of HIV-1 was diagnosed in Ghana in 1986 in a Ghanaian couple who lived Germany and were returning to Ghana for a vacation. The HIV-1 is rare in West Africa, but HIV-2 is common in West Africa from Nigeria to Senegal; whereas, HIV–1 is common in the Western world of America and Europe where HIV-2 is rare.

The diverse forms of HIV is evident from the historical findings and the fact that the HIV virus has a lot of mechanisms to change and will change to virulent forms when it gets the opportunity. This is evident from the historical narrative of medical research. HIV's innate ability to change makes it difficult for scientists and medical researchers to find a vaccine and a cure for HIV. Nobody knows for sure as to what precipitated a shift from nonvirulent forms of HIV to the virulent forms of subtype B of the group M strain of HIV, which is causing the present HIV-1 epidemic and then the reason why HIV-2 epidemic is limited to West Africa.

Our behaviors might have allowed us to come into contact with nonvirulent forms of HIV and further transfer of the HIV in places of the human body where the virus was more likely to be nourished and mutate into virulent forms of HIV-1 and HIV-2. In order for us not be biased about the origin of the HIV epidemic, the ongoing studies in Africa need to be duplicated in other places in the world where virulent forms of HIV were described in the early 1980s to find out if HIV had existed in those communities for a longer time and how such people who died from the early phase of the epidemic might have come into contact with the virulent forms of HIV-1 and HIV-2. Perhaps such studies can help us to find strains of the HIV virus that are much more similar to the virulent strains of HIV-1 and HIV-2 than those described in Leopoldville, which may then facilitate HIV vaccine production.

Why is it that HIV-1 was described in men who have sex with men at the onset of the HIV epidemic in the U.S. and later in Europe and also HIV-2 was described to be limited to West Africa where the heterosexual mode of transmission from men to women or women to men remained the dominant mode of infection?

The following scientific news articles discuss the origin of HIV infection in the search for answers to the HIV epidemic. The first excerpt is an original narrative of scientific findings about the existence of diverse forms of HIV.

HIV Existed 100 Years Ago Study Reports, Urbanization of Africa Spread HIV Then

The urbanization of Africa in the early part of the 20th century may be partly responsible for the spread of HIV. The suggestion was derived from an analysis of a tissue sample taken in 1960 in what was then Leopoldville, the colonial capital of the Belgian Congo, according to Michael Worobey, D. Phil., of the University of Arizona, and colleagues.

HIV RNA taken from the sample, which had been fixed in paraffin, provided the second oldest viral sequence, next to one from a blood sample—also from Leopoldville—taken in 1959.

The key finding is that the two samples—both of HIV-1 Group M—are sufficiently different that their earliest common ancestor must have existed about 50 years previously.

At that time, Leopoldville—and most population centers in central Africa—was small, providing only a small pool in which HIV could spread. But as the cities grew, HIV diversified, the researchers suggested. [medpagetoday.com]

"The interpretation that HIV-1 was spreading among humans for 60–80 years before AIDS was first recognized should not be surprising. If the epidemic grew roughly exponentially from only one or a few infected individuals around 1910 to the more than 55 million estimated to have been infected by 2007, there were probably only a few thousand HIV-infected individuals by 1960, all in central Africa. Given the diverse array of symptoms characteristic of AIDS, and the often-long asymptomatic period following infection, it is easy to imagine how the nascent epidemic went unrecognized. Conversely, such a low prevalence at that time implies that the

Congolese co-authors of the paper were very lucky to come across this infected sample, even if most infections were concentrated in the area of Léopoldville. But can we trust these sequences? ... it seems likely that all of the early diversification of HIV-1 group M viruses occurred in the Léopoldville area ... Léopoldville was not only the largest of these cities, but also a likely destination for a virus escaping from southeast Cameroon. In the early 1900s, the main routes of transportation out of that remote forest region were rivers; those surrounding this area flow south, ultimately draining into the Congo River, and leading to Léopoldville ... The date estimates of Worobey et al. are for an ancestral virus, present in the first individual to give rise to separate transmission chains that still exist today. We may never know how many individuals were infected in the previous transmission chain, the one that led from the person initially infected with SIV to the progenitor of the current pandemic in humans." (Sharp, 2008). Reprinted by permission from Macmillan Publishers Ltd: Journal NATURE 455, 661-664 October 2, 2008. Original source: Michael Worobey et al. Direct evidence of extensive diversity of HIV-1 in Kinshasa by 1960, copyright © 2008.

Tissue sample suggests HIV has been infecting humans for a century

48-year-old lymph node biopsy reveals the history of the deadly virus.

Heidi Ledford

A biopsy taken from an African woman nearly 50 years ago contains traces of the HIV genome, researchers have found. Analysis of sequences from the newly discovered sample suggests that the virus has been plaguing humans for almost a century.

Although AIDS was not recognized until the 1980s, HIV was infecting humans well before then. Researchers hope that by studying the origin and evolution of HIV, they can learn more about how the virus made the leap from chimpanzees to humans, and work out how best to design a vaccine to fight it.

In 1998, researchers reported the isolation of HIV-1 sequences from a blood sample taken in 1959 from a Bantu male living in Léopoldville—now Kinshasa, the capital of the Democratic Republic of the Congo. Analysis of that sample and others suggested that HIV-1 originates from sometime between 1915 and 1941.

Now, researchers report in Nature that they have uncovered another historic sample, collected in 1960 from a woman who also lived in Léopoldville.

It took evolutionary biologist Michael Worobey of the University of Arizona in Tucson and his colleagues eight years of searching for suitable tissue collections originating in Africa before they tracked down the 1960 lymph node biopsy at the University of Kinshasa.

Drenched in glue

The samples had all been treated with harsh chemicals, embedded in paraffin wax and left at room temperature for decades. The acidic chemicals had broken the genome up into small fragments. Formalin, a chemical used to prepare samples for microscopy, had crosslinked nucleic acids with protein. "It's as if you had a nice pearl necklace of DNA and RNA and protein and you clumped it together, drenched it in glue and then dried it out," says Worobey.

The team worked out a combination of methods that would allow them to sequence DNA and RNA from the samples; another lab at Northwestern University in Chicago, Illinois, confirmed the results, also finding traces of the HIV-1 genome in the lymph node biopsy.

Kinshasa was founded around 1885. The growth of Kinshasa and other cities in the region may have been crucial to the emergence of HIV/AIDS, according to the Royal Museum for Central Africa.

Using a database of HIV-1 sequences and an estimate of the rate at which these sequences change over time, the researchers modelled when HIV-1 first surfaced. Their results showed that the most likely date for HIV's emergence was about 1908, when Léopoldville was emerging as a centre for trade.

Although that date will not surprise most HIV researchers, the new data should help persuade those who were unconvinced by the 1959 sample, says Beatrice Hahn, an HIV researcher at the University of Alabama at Birmingham.

The sequences of the 1959 and 1960 samples—the earliest

that have ever been found—show a difference of about 12%. "This shows very clearly that there was tremendous variation even then," says Simon Wain-Hobson, a virologist at the Pasteur Institute in Paris.

A virus ready for its close-up

However, it may never be possible to pinpoint exactly how HIV crossed from chimpanzees into humans, Hahn cautions. She and her collaborators previously tracked the likely source of HIV-1 to chimpanzees living in southeast Cameroon, hundreds of kilometres from Kinshasa, and it is tempting to hypothesize that trade routes contributed to the virus's infiltration of the city. But even by 1960, HIV-1 had infected only a few thousand Africans. It is unlikely that it will be possible to track down samples from the very earliest victims, Hahn notes.

Meanwhile, Worobey plans to continue his search through old tissue collections in the hope of finding additional samples. In time, he says, it may even be possible to reconstruct the historic HIV viruses for further study.

Collecting information about old strains of HIV—even those that disappeared over time—can help researchers learn how successful strains broke through, says Wain-Hobson. "For every star in Hollywood there are fifty starlets," he says. "We would love to know what it was that caused this strain to move out of starlet phase and to the big time." (Nature, published online, Oct. 1, 2008). Reprinted by permission from Macmillan Publishers Ltd:

NATURE NEWS, October 1, 2008. Original source: Michael Worobey et al. Direct evidence of extensive diversity of HIV-1 in Kinshasa by 1960, copyright © 2008.

AIDS: Prehistory of HIV-1

Paul M. Sharp and Beatrice H. Hahn

The origin of the current AIDS pandemic has been a subject of great interest and speculation. Viral archaeology sheds light on the geography and timescale of the early diversification of HIV-1 in humans.

Human immunodeficiency virus type 1 (HIV-1) must have been spreading through the human population long before AIDS was first described in 1981, but very few strains from this 'prehistoric' period (pre-1980s) have been characterized. Viral sequences from earlier times can provide insight into the early spread of HIV-1, because the rapid rate of evolution of this virus—up to a million times faster than that of animal DNA—means that substantial amounts of sequence change occur in a matter of decades. On page 661 of this issue, Worobey et al. describe the sequences of partial genome fragments of HIV-1 from a lymph-node biopsy collected in 1960 in Léopoldville (now Kinshasa, Democratic Republic of the Congo). They compare these sequences with those of other HIV-1 strains, shedding light on the early evolution and diversification of this virus in Africa.

HIV-1 strains are divided into three groups, each of which was independently derived from a simian immunodeficiency virus (SIV) that naturally infects

chimpanzees in west-central Africa. Whereas two of
these groups are rare, the third, group M, has spread
throughout the world and is the cause of more than 95%
of HIV infections globally. Group M can be further
divided into many subtypes (A–K), which seem to have
arisen through founder events. For example, subtype B,
which encompasses all the strains originally described in
North America and Europe, is very rare in Africa, and
reflects such a founder event. Last year, Worobey and
colleagues showed that this subtype probably arose from
a single strain that was carried from Africa to Haiti before
spreading to the United States and onwards. The newly
described 1960 virus (DRC60) falls within, but close to
the ancestor of, subtype A.

DRC60 is not the first "ancient" HIV-1 sample to be
characterized: viral sequences from a blood-plasma sample
originally obtained in 1959—also from Léopoldville—
were published 10 years ago. The importance of DRC60
is that it is highly divergent from the 1959 sample
(ZR59), which was most closely related to the ancestor
of subtype D, thus directly demonstrating that, by 50
years ago, group M HIV-1 strains had already undergone
substantial diversification.

The ZR59 and DRC60 sequences differ by about 12%,
a value similar to distances now seen between the most
divergent strains within subtypes. As the positions of
ZR59 and DRC60 within the group M phylogeny
indicate that the various subtypes already existed 50
years ago, simple extrapolation suggests that these two

viral sequences had a common ancestor at least 50 years before that. For a more robust estimate of the date of the common ancestor of HIV-1 group M strains, Worobey and colleagues used state-of-the-art statistical analyses, allowing a variety of models for the growth of the HIV-1 pandemic and variable rates of evolution. The different analyses gave broadly similar estimates for the date of that common ancestor, between 1902 and 1921, with 95% confidence intervals ranging no later than 1933. These dates are a little earlier than, but do not differ significantly from, a previous estimate of 1931 from an analysis that did not include the 50-year-old viruses.

The interpretation that HIV-1 was spreading among humans for 60–80 years before AIDS was first recognized should not be surprising. If the epidemic grew roughly exponentially from only one or a few infected individuals around 1910 to the more than 55 million estimated to have been infected by 2007, there were probably only a few thousand HIV-infected individuals by 1960, all in central Africa. Given the diverse array of symptoms characteristic of AIDS, and the often-long asymptomatic period following infection, it is easy to imagine how the nascent epidemic went unrecognized. Conversely, such a low prevalence at that time implies that the Congolese co-authors of the paper were very lucky to come across this infected sample, even if most infections were concentrated in the area of Léopoldville. But can we trust these sequences?

In work on ancient DNA, contamination is especially

problematic, and the work should, if possible, be replicated in other laboratories. For DRC60, independent analyses were performed at the University of Arizona and Northwestern University, Illinois. The sequences obtained were similar, but not identical, exactly as expected when samples come from the diverse set of related viral sequences that—because of the virus's rapid rate of evolution—arise within an infected individual. Furthermore, the distance along the evolutionary tree from the group M ancestor to the ZR59 or DRC60 sequences is much shorter than those between the ancestor and modern strains, consistent with the earlier dates of isolation of ZR59 and DRC60, and confirming that these viruses are indeed old.

Although the ZR59 and DRC60 sequences can show only that two subtypes were present in Léopoldville around 1960, in more recent times the greatest diversity of group M subtypes—as well as many divergent strains that have not been classified—has been found in Kinshasa. So it seems likely that all of the early diversification of HIV-1 group M viruses occurred in the Léopoldville area. Yet the SIV strains most closely related to HIV-1 group M have been found infecting chimpanzees in the southeast corner of Cameroon, some 700 kilometres away. The simplest explanation for how SIV jumped to humans would be through exposure of humans to the blood of chimpanzees butchered locally for bushmeat. So why did the pandemic start in Léopoldville? And, as there must have been many opportunities for such transmission over past millennia, why did the AIDS pandemic not occur until the twentieth century? (Sharp, 2008). Reprinted by permission from Macmillan Publishers Ltd: Journal NATURE October 1, 2008. Original Sources: Paul M. Sharp, Beatrice H. Hahn and Michael Worobey et al. Copyright © 2008

The information about the origin of HIV is an interesting scientific finding and excellent work. It is most probable that the earlier forms of HIV described in Leopoldville were nonvirulent. Maybe we need to find out the conditions and situations that can precipitate a change of nonvirulent HIV virus to virulent forms and the HIV genotype that is almost similar to the genotype of the subtypes B of the group M strain of HIV. It may happen that, when we get to know how such a change could have occurred from nonvirulent to the epidemic forms of virulent HIV-1 and HIV-2, we might be able to formulate a vaccine and treatment for a cure. Maybe we could prevent similar conditions from causing other forms of HIV epidemic in the future.

[B] Prevention of HIV epidemic

What can be done to prevent the HIV spread by HIV positive patients?

In addition to the individual HIV prevention action discussed in chapter four, every person is encouraged to adopt an STD/HIV behavior modification plan and help prevent the spread of HIV infection. The CDC has developed a strategy called Serostatus Approach to Fighting the HIV Epidemic (SAFE).

The SAFE HIV prevention plan must be used to prevent those who have HIV from spreading HIV and to help those who do have HIV live a healthy life by complying with their medical treatment. The five key steps called 5 SAFE steps are as follows:

1. Increase the number of HIV infected persons who know their HIV positive test results (serostatus).

2. Increase use of healthcare services and prevention services.

3. Increase high quality care and treatment.

4. Increase adherence to therapy by individuals with HIV infection.

5. Increase the number of individuals with HIV who adopt and sustain STD/HIV risk reduction behavior.

It is not uncommon to find that HIV/AIDS patients have additional STDs after they are aware that they are HIV positive. Such behavior is an indicator of the spread of HIV infection. There are various evidence-based behavior modification models recommended by the CDC for implementation at STD/HIV clinics to prevent exposure and transmission of STDs such as VOICES/VOCES, Partnership for Health and Comprehensive Risk Counseling and Services (CRCS).

VOICES/VOCES is a single-session, video-based HIV/STD prevention workshop designed to encourage condom use and improve condom negotiation skills among African American and Latino adults and has been found to consistently increase knowledge about the transmission of HIV and other STDs, provide a more realistic assessment of their personal risk, and show greater likelihood of getting condoms and intending to use them regularly and fewer repeat STD infections (Sweat 2001).

Partnership for Health is a three-to-five minutes HIV risk behavior intervention administered by physicians to HIV-positive patients at the clinic. It was done by researches from Keck School of Medicine, University of Southern California and University of California at San Diego in the U.S. They found out that, patients who have two or more sex partners and received three-to-five minutes counseling from physicians about the negative consequences of unsafe sex, reduced unprotected sex by 38% during a periods of ten-to- eleven months and the finding was statistically significant. The importance of the functions of physicians to help their patients to protect themselves and prevent contact with STD/HIV is vital to HIV/AIDS control. Public Health programs must help to implement HIV/AIDS preventions right from the doctor's office.

Doctors and public health services must develop plans to encourage the HIV patients to give their sex partners the chance to protect themselves and use condoms for all sexual activities when they decide to have sex. HIV positive patients who behave in such a manner to spread HIV infection must be reminded about the laws of the land concerning the need for sex behavior modification to protect others from being exposed to HIV.

HIV positive patients are required by law to inform their doctor, dentist, and sex partner of their positive results. They cannot donate blood and blood products. They are encouraged to clean spills of body fluids such as blood and urine with detergents and must not share body piercing needles and syringes and sharp personal objects like razors, knives, and blades. When they decide to have sex, they must always use condoms.

A surveillance for individuals known to have been exposed to HIV infection by sex, needle sharing, occupational exposure, blood products exposure, and breastfeeding should be encouraged to do follow-up testing by three to six months after initial negative HIV test. Anyone exposed will benefit from treatment. It's better than not knowing about seroconvertion to HIV positive status and unknowingly transmitting HIV infection to other sex partners and developing AIDS and its related complications, financial burden, suffering, and early death.

Testing for STD/HIV regularly by six to twelve months is important for every sexually active person and those whose lifestyles put them at risk of getting STD/HIV. Always don't forget to test together with your would-be sex partner no matter the person's previous HIV test results, and verify HIV test results to make sure it is negative before making a decision about when to have sex. It will help you to make informed decisions and avoid having unprotected sex with a person who is known to be HIV positive and those who already have HIV infection but may not be aware that they are HIV positive.

The government and policymakers, churches, community leaders, chiefs, and kings have responsibility to play an active role in the prevention and intervention of the spread of HIV infection. It is critical to reduce suffering of populations significantly affected by HIV infection. Since the spread of HIV now is mainly by sexual exposure, changes in the population dynamics of the infection should be expected. Therefore, everybody could be affected directly or indirectly now and in the future. Until a vaccine and treatment to cure is found, HIV prevention should be an individual, family, and national priority.

Unfortunately, many have underestimated the smartness of HIV—a virus that can utilize human DNA to produce more proteins and multiply themselves and can change to new forms that could resist the ability of known multiple medications like HAART. Public health workers and physicians need to work with known HIV positive patients who continue to ignore safer sex by informing their sex partner about their HIV status and do not use protective condoms consistently to avoid the transmission and spread of HIV. Such HIV positive patients may even exchange different forms of HIV knowingly and unknowingly with HIV positive partner(s). Such behaviors have been documented among men who have sex with men (MSM) in New York, where original cases of HIV were noted in 1981 and have been associated with resistant forms (strain) of HIV with rapid progression to AIDS (CDC 2006).

Men who cannot quit having sex with men have the responsibility to protect each other by informing their partners of their status and using condoms always. Such a responsibility has been ignored by many of them for a long time even after twenty-five years of HIV infection. Many more MSM continue to get HIV and syphilis infections at a faster rate than any other group of sex partners. It is not good that men are killing men with HIV infection. That is not an act of love. It is also not good when such men are killing women and infants with HIV by their bisexual behavior. Let's protect each other as a true demonstration of love and responsibility.

According to a CDC yearly incidence report, an estimated 54,230 new infections occurred in 2006 among whites, blacks, and Hispanics by analysis of reports from twenty-two states in the U.S. Also, 73 percent of new infections of HIV in the U.S. were in males, and for these new infections among males, 72 percent were MSM. Overall, 45 percent of the new HIV infections were blacks and 53 percent were MSM (CDC 2008).

Protection of females from HIV especially black and Hispanic females, must be urgent. The public health departments, doctors, nurses, NGOs, CBOs, and governments must find ways to prevent the high rate of HIV infection among men in the U.S. from spreading to women and especially among black women because high risk heterosexual contacts accounted for 80 percent of new HIV infections among females and 13 percent among men (CDC 2008). More women get HIV infection from heterosexual relationships with men. More men get HIV infection from sex with men.

Among females, 61 percent of new infections were in blacks, and black females have an incidence rate of 14.7 times the rate for white females. Hispanic females had 16 percent of new HIV infections and 3.8 times the rate for white females (CDC 2008).

Thus, bisexual men who hide their identity from women may be contributing to the new trend of increasing HIV infection in women especially among black and Hispanic women in the U.S. The only way to find out is to test for HIV infection and know the results before sex, and females must make testing for HIV a requirement and a responsible act of love and commitment from men before having sex. Many women have thought of condoms to protect them from HIV but failed to use them consistently with all sex partners all the time and got HIV infection.

Age has impact on HIV epidemic. The age group 13–29 years needs special attention especially among black and Hispanic MSM.

New infections of HIV among black and Hispanic MSM aged 13–29 years is high (CDC 2008). Special consideration for age appropriate intervention is important. Good surveillance reports and analysis that are more applicable for intervention are essential.

Globally, the confidential reporting of all cases and yearly HIV incidence reports by all counties, regions, states, and countries must be enforced by all government policies to enable doctors, public health workers, and laboratories' health scientists to study the dynamics of the spread of HIV within every community. It will help to formulate intervention methods to limit HIV epidemics before it gets out of control in subgroups of the populations.

A continuous mass education of HIV transmission and prevention is vital for the entire world and communities to understand how to limit the spread of the disease process, for treatment of HIV patients to stay healthy, and for the acceptance of HIV patients as people who need support and care. The responsibility of the government and the community to support people who made mistakes directly or indirectly and got HIV as well as those who accidentally got infected with HIV will be embraced when people are well informed and understand the disease transmission process. This may help to break the silence of HIV positive patients relocating to other places and spreading HIV infection. HIV positive patients and their supportive family and community must know that by telling the sex partner of being HIV positive they help to limit the spread of HIV infection since HIV does not spread by casual contact like hand shaking and eating at the same table with an HIV patient.

Everyone should therefore break the culture of silence and talk about HIV prevention and get to know their HIV test results. Schools, communities, and religious faiths like churches must accept continuous lifetime HIV health education. Governments must make it a policy to continue HIV mass education and make sure that everybody gets the chance to understand how to stop the spread of HIV as a means of keeping the society healthy.

We assume that people know a lot about how to protect themselves from STD/HIV, but the fact is that these diseases are associated with passions and behavior choice that a lot of people find very difficult to control. Besides, unprotected sex is a process that enables families to continue their existence and will continue to be part of our life. Therefore, continuous STD/HIV awareness and education is essential throughout every person's life so that people will understand how they and others can get STD/HIV infection. They need to understand the fact that HIV is not spread by casual contact and that when people get tested to know their HIV positive results, they should stop using drugs and sharing needles and syringes. If they stop, they limit the process of passing the disease to other people and stop the spread of HIV.

The culture of silence about HIV positive results and not telling sex partners of HIV positive results must be discouraged and stopped. HIV positive people must protect every person they claim to love since they will need such people to directly or indirectly support and help take care of them when they are sick. And they have a responsibility to help the government, friends, families, and health care workers to take care of them and stop the spread of HIV infection.

From the CDC report of HIV incidence by 2006, it is obvious that behavior, cultural, gender, and age-specific HIV prevention and intervention methods and safer sex by using condoms consistently by known sexually active HIV positive patients especially MSM must be actively pursued to limit the spread of HIV infection. Stratification of such HIV prevention and intervention methods—when combined with sustained individualized prevention action plans and the already existing generalized HIV prevention education and methods of avoiding contact with HIV such as abstinence, being faithfully committed to one sex partner in monogamy, and consistent condom use "ABC"—may be a more effective approach to prevent and control the HIV epidemic.

Stratification of HIV prevention intervention into sexual transmission prevention, intravenous transmission prevention, and perinatal transmission prevention has been proposed by Valdiserri et al. in a book, *Nature Medicine 2003*, based on clinical evidence. Thus small group behavioral intervention, counseling and testing, community level interventions, structural interventions, STD diagnosis and treatment have been found by clinical studies to prevent sexual transmission of HIV infection.

Intravenous transmission of HIV can be prevented by blood safety, occupation setting precautions, injection drug use programs applying behavioral change interventions, drug treatment, and access to sterile injection equipment.

Pharmaceutical interventions using zidovudine and nevirapine and breast-milk supplementation depending on local circumstances have been used to reduce perinatal transmission of HIV infection.

Though the scientific approach helps to some extent, however, none of them can replace individual commitment to unconditionally love one person and unconditionally respect and commit sex life to only one person who will also unconditionally commit in the same manner to you as described in the teachings of the Jewish and the Christian faith in the Bible. It is clearly evident that married couples who believed and practiced what the Jewish and the Christian God teaches about sex life before marriage and continued to remain committed to unconditionally love and sexually commit to only their spouse have remained protected from sexual transmission of HIV infection. Those who do not believe in the kind of sexual relationship described by God through selected men and prophets in the Bible cannot practice it, and they generalize it and say that it does not work.

It is quite evident that for the period after World War II, there has been so much scientific and medical technology and advancement and prosperity in most parts of the world, yet men and women have stubbornly chosen sexual behaviors that are self-centered and self-destructive, with less value on life and the well-being of others. Some are willing to adopt a lifestyle that is sex and drug dependent leading to STD/HIV, early HIV infection during the active years of their life, suffering from HIV/AIDS and early death. You should not be surprised to find how accurate the Bible has been in predicting what will happen when men and women behave in the manner we find ourselves now as imperfect perishable mortals.

[B] Jewish and Christian faith in God could limit HIV epidemic

Approximately 75 percent of the men and women with acquired immunodeficiency syndrome in the United States as of 2006 were infected through sexual contact, making interventions aimed at reducing risky sexual behavior important for HIV infection prevention and control (CDC 2008). In the developing countries where the use of intravenous drug abuse is not a problem, many more men and women acquire HIV/AIDS through sexual contact. Information that will help people willing to adopt a life of commitment to only one sex partner will be helpful to avoid risky sexual behaviors that eventually lead to HIV. Information to avoid prolonged diseases with associated high medical costs and disability, suffering, and early death is definitely needed to limit the spread of HIV infection and epidemic.

There is no book on earth that can be compared to the Bible for its ability to predict the future and the consequences of our sexual behavior. It will be the source to help people willing to adopt a life of commitment to only one sex partner through marriage. Without marriage, a commitment to one sex partner virtually fails, and at the time of failure STD/HIV could be the end result.

In my search for answers, I have found that many have ignored or do not know the following quotations about our sex life and many others from the Bible that accurately predict the consequences of not getting committed to only one sexual partner in marriage as the only means to continue to be sexually active yet avoid problems and deadly diseases like HIV, hepatitis B, and hepatitis C. However, to avoid getting HIV at the onset of a committed sexual relationship like marriage, it is advisable to always test your would-be marriage partner for HIV, hepatitis B, hepatitis C, gonorrhea, chlamydia, and syphilis before marriage. Many have made mistakes by not committing to only one sex partner in marriage, and they are either seriously sick or died prematurely from HIV infection.

Please read these Bible quotations about sexual life, adopt and maintain the healthy advice, and you will find answers to preventing HIV infection if you consistently and faithfully practice what it says. Find a wife or husband who will consistently and faithfully obey these truths in the Bible as revealed through men of God from the Old Testament to the New Testament. I searched quotations from the *New King James Bible.*

In the old testament of the Bible, King Solomon reveals to us that sexual immorality with a person who has multiple sex partners, a "harlot," also known as a prostitute, can lead to death. This advice can be found in Proverbs 7:6–23. "For at the window of my house I looked through my lattice, and saw among the youths, a young man devoid of understanding, passing along the street near her corner; And he took the path to her house in the twilight, in the evening, in the black and dark night. And there a woman met him, with the attire of a harlot, and a crafty heart. She was loud and rebellious, her feet would not stay at home. At times she was outside, at times in the open square, lurking at every corner. So she caught him and kissed him; with an impudent face she said to him; 'I have peace offerings with me; Today, I have paid my vows. So I came out to meet you, Diligently to seek your face, And I have found you. I have spread my bed with tapestry, colored covering of Egyptian linen. I have perfumed my bed with myrrh, aloes and cinnamon. Come let us take our fill of love until morning; Let us delight ourselves with love. For my husband is not at home; He has gone on a long journey; He has taken a bag of money with him, And will come home on the appointed day.' With her enticing speech she caused him to yield, with her flattering lips she seduced him. Immediately he went after her, as an ox goes to the slaughter, Or as a fool to the correction of the stocks, till an arrow struck his liver. As a bird hastens to the snare, he did not know it would cost his life."

This is King Solomon's advice Proverbs 7:24–27. "Now therefore, listen to me, my children; Pay attention to the words of my mouth: Do not let your heart turn aside to her ways, Do not stray into her paths; For she has cast down many wounded, And all who were slain by her were strong men, Her house is a way to hell, Descending to the chambers of death."

This advice is very important if anyone wants to prevent getting HIV/AIDS. HIV is more common in male and female prostitutes and their sex partners according to the scientific literature of STD/HIV.

Later on, King Solomon made a mistake by marrying many women in polygamy, and some of the wives led him astray and made him believe in their gods and the consequences were not good. And he said, "Vanity of vanity, all is vanity" (Ecclesiastes 1:2).

The Bible also gives us examples that when people make a mistake and have sex outside marriage, they can die within a short time. But when they change their behavior quickly enough, confessed to God and ask for forgiveness, God will forgive them (1 John 1:8-10). If they do not commit such behavior again, they are forgiven indeed, live and be blessed. King David is a typical example of such mercies from God.

From the Old Testament documentation, King David confessed his sin after he made a mistake and committed adultery with Bathsheba, the wife of Uriah, and God forgave him. From the reading of 2 Samuel 12:9–13, Nathan, the prophet, was sent by God to David and he told

David: "Why have you despised the commandment of the Lord, to do evil in His sight? You have killed Uriah the Hittite with the sword; you have taken his wife to be your wife, and have killed him with the sword of the people of Ammon. 'Now therefore, the sword shall never depart from your house, because you have despised Me, and have taken the wife of Uriah the Hittite to be your wife.' 'Thus says the Lord: Behold, I will raise up adversity against you from your own house: and I will take your wives before your eyes and give them to your neighbor, and he shall lie with your wives in the sight of this sun. For you did it secretly, but I will do this thing before all Israel, before the sun." So David said to Nathan. "I have sin against the Lord," And Nathan said to David, "The Lord also has put away your sin; you shall not die."

King David was indeed blessed and through his ancestry, Jesus was born and he changed the entire world by his power to heal people with all kinds of diseases, love people irrespective of their nature and background and by faith his death reconcile man to God.

Look at what Jesus said to the woman caught in adultery. If for any reason someone is in a sexual relationship with a person who is not the wife or husband, the Bible calls it a sin. We can confess our sins, and God will forgive us and gives us a new beginning to accept and follow what His word directs us to do—that is, to abstain from any kind of sexual relationship until marriage.

Jesus reminded us about this when a woman was caught in adultery and was brought before him. This can be found in the New Testament of the Bible from John 8:2–12. Now early in the morning, He (Jesus) came again into the temple, and all the people came to Him; and He sat down and taught them. Then the scribes and the Pharisees brought to him a woman caught in adultery. And when they had set her in the midst, they said to Him, 'Teacher, this woman was caught in adultery, in the very act. Now Moses in the law commanded us that such should be stoned. But what do you say?' This they said, testing Him, that they might have something of which to accuse Him. But Jesus stooped down and wrote on the ground with His finger, as though He did not hear. So when they continued asking Him, He raised Himself up and said to them, 'He who is without sin among you, let him throw a stone at her first.' And again, He stooped down and wrote on the ground. Then those who heard it, being convicted by their conscience, went out one by one, beginning with the oldest even to the last. And Jesus was left alone, and the woman standing in the midst. When Jesus had raised Himself up and saw no one but the woman, He said to her, 'Woman, where are those accusers of yours? Has no one condemned you?' She said. 'No one, Lord.' And Jesus said to her, neither do I condemn you; go and sin no more. Then Jesus spoke to them again, saying, 'I am the light of the world, He who follows Me shall not walk in darkness, but have the light of life.'

Applying what Jesus said to the present world of STDs and HIV/AIDS, if anyone follows what He said and repents from adultery and sexual sin, the person shall save his or her life and also the life of family and friends from living in the darkness of the disease of STDs and HIV/AIDS.

The need to protect others from infectious diseases has its roots in the Bible. When the Israelites were on their journey through the wilderness, God demonstrated his love and power to care about them, love and protect them, as an example to all of us. He also revealed to them what they should do to protect themselves when someone gets an infectious disease. This can be found in Numbers 5:1–4. "And the Lord spoke to Moses, saying: 'Command the children of the Israel that they put out of the camp every leper, everyone who has a discharge and whoever becomes defiled by a corpse. You shall put out both male and female; you shall put them outside the camp, that they may not defile their camps in the midst of which I dwell.' And the children of Israel did so, and put them outside the camp; as the Lord spoke to Moses, so the children of Israel did."

These people that the Lord told Moses to separate from the camp had infectious diseases like leprosy as described by the Bible. They were reminded to cover themselves and to remind other people that they were infectious so that people will not come too close to them at a time they had no cure for the disease. This was a very important disease prevention method at that time.

From the previous Biblical narrative at Numbers 5:1–4, it is certain that God knew that the diseases those people had were infectious and could be passed on to others. At that time He had not revealed what germs can cause these diseases, but He demonstrated His power to heal those diseases by miraculous healing of lepers by prophets like Elisha (2 kings 5:1-17) and then by Jesus (Luke 17:11-19), whom the Bible refers to as the son of God. Current medical practice applies the same wisdom to put people with infectious diseases like tuberculosis and leprosy in isolation until they have taken enough medications to make them less likely to pass on the infection to others.

Centuries after this wisdom of isolating people who had infectious diseases, a church worker, Robert Hooke, who worked in the monastery made an outstanding discovery by using a microscope to look at the building blocks of every living thing called the "cells." This discovery made us aware that people get infectious diseases because of small organisms called bacteria, virus, fungi, protozoa, and others. DNA and RNA, which modern medicine has been working on as the basis of cell division and multiplication and organisms as a whole and its association with certain diseases when some things go wrong in the process of cell division and multiplication are inside the cell, which was discovered by the monastery scientist Robert Hooke (1635–1703). As explained already, HIV is RNA virus that has the ability to use human DNA to produce more HIV virus. Could such a discovery in the monastery and what the Bible tells us about infectious diseases be something known by God? If yes, can't we follow what the Bible says and avoid HIV infection?

An apostle and teacher of God called Paul—a man who initially persecuted Christians until he had a personal encounter with the resurrected Jesus and was transformed and renewed to believe in the teachings of God through Jesus Christ and then empowered by God to bring the word of God to non-Jewish nations—wrote most of the contents of the New Testament of the Bible. Apostle Paul revealed to us that when people ignore the existence of God and the purity of human creation, their behavior can change, and such people adopt behaviors including men having sex with men and women having sex with women, and then they received penalty for their error. He also said that such behaviors lead to death. Could HIV infection and many other behavior problems associated with suffering and early death be part of the prophesy by Apostle Paul being fulfilled now? Let us read the following Bible quotations carefully and think about what Apostle Paul said in Hebrews 13:4. "Marriage is honorable among all, and the bed undefiled; but fornicators and adulterers God will judge."

And in Romans 12:1–2, "I beseech you therefore brethren, by the mercies of God, that you present your bodies a living sacrifice, holy, acceptable to God, which is your reasonable service. And do not be conformed to this word but be transformed by the renewing of your mind, that you may prove what is that good and acceptable and perfect will of God." Then in Romans 1:18–32, Paul said, "For the wrath of God is revealed from Heaven against all ungodliness and unrighteousness of men, who suppress the truth in righteousness, because what may be known of God is manifest in them, for God has shown it to them. For since the creation of the world, His invisible attributes are clearly seen, being understood by the things that are made, even His eternal power and Godhead, so that they are without excuse, because, although they knew God, they did not glorify Him as God, nor were thankful, but became futile in their thoughts, and their foolish hearts were darkened. Professing to be wise, they became fools, and changed the glory of the incorruptible God into an image made like corruptible man and birds and four-footed animals and creeping things. Therefore God also gave them up to uncleanness, in lusts of their hearts, to dishonor their bodies among themselves, who exchanged the truth of God for the lie, and worshiped and served the creature rather than the Creator, who is blessed forever, Amen. For this reason God gave them up to vile passions. For even their women exchanged the natural use for what is against nature. Likewise also the men, leaving the natural use of the woman, burned in their lust for one another, men with men committing what is shameful and receiving in themselves the penalty of their error which was due. And even as they did not like to retain God in their knowledge, God gave them over to debased mind, to do those things which are not fitting; being filled with all unrighteousness, sexual immorality, wickedness, covetousness, maliciousness; full of envy, murder, strife, deceit, evil-mindedness; they are whisperers, backbiters, haters of God, violent, proud, boasters, inventors of evil things, disobedient to parents, undiscerning, untrustworthy, unloving, unforgiving, unmerciful; who knowing the righteous judgement of God, that those who practice such things are deserving of death, not only do the same but also approve of those who practice them."

Many people with HIV have found love and peace and joy by making changes and accepting the attribute of God to forgive and heal them spiritually. When I researched and found the words written by King David in Psalm 103, I was not surprised to find that even people who made mistakes in their sexual lifestyle and got HIV infection but made changes in their behavior and lifestyle and have accepted God and adopted beliefs and practices in the Bible have been transformed to live a life of peace and determination, compliant with their treatment so they could live. Such HIV positive patients are always ready to tell other people that they are HIV positive. They do not spread HIV infection and will not put other people at risk of getting HIV infection. They are ready to assist other people living with HIV/AIDS to make adjustments to their sexual lifestyle.

Let us read what the Bible says about such people who have accepted God even after making mistakes and also about other God-fearing and obedient believers after getting diseases. Psalm 103 quoted from the *New King James Bible*: "Bless the Lord, O my soul; And all that is within me, bless His holy name. Bless the Lord, O my soul, and forget not all His benefit: Who forgives all your iniquities, Who heals all your diseases, Who redeems your life from destruction, Who crowns you with the loving kindness and tender mercies, Who satisfies your mouth with good things, so that your youth is renewed like eagle's. The LORD executes righteousness and justice for all who are oppressed, He made known His ways to Moses, His acts to the children of Israel. The Lord is merciful and gracious, slow to anger and abounding in mercy, He will not always strive with us, Nor will He keep His anger forever. He has not dealt with us according to our sins, Nor punished us according to our iniquities. For as heavens are high above the earth, so great is His mercy toward those who fear Him; As far as the east is from the west, So far has He removed our transgressions from us. As a father pities his children, So the Lord pities those who fear Him. For He knows our frame; He remembers that we are dust. As for man, his days are like grass; As a flower of the field, so he flourishes. For the wind passes over it, and it is gone. And its place remembers it no more. But the mercy of the Lord is from everlasting to everlasting On those who fear Him, And His righteousness to children's children, To such as keep His covenant, And to those who remember His commandments to do them. The Lord has established His throne in heaven, And His kingdom rules over all. Bless the Lord, you His angels, Who excel in strength, who do His word, Heeding the voice of His word. Bless the Lord, all you His hosts, You ministers of His, who do his pleasure. Bless the Lord, all His works, In all places of His dominion. Bless the Lord, O my soul!"

From the Bible literature research and the information found, I think the Jewish and Christian God has a special message for us to keep us protected from getting STD/HIV; therefore, the believers must always remember to pray to God to help us find a cure for HIV infection. Churches obviously have a vital duty to help people avoid coming into contact with STD/HIV infection.

Jesus knew the importance of commitment to only one sex partner by the process of marriage of a man to a woman. Jesus said the only time a man can divorce a woman is when she commits adultery. Adultery is the only basis for divorce in marriage. It is obvious that He said this to protect everybody. The hardness of heart makes people not love, care, and stay committed to only one sex partner and then divorce.

Let us look at what Jesus said from Mark 10:1–9, when he was questioned about writing a certificate of divorce in a marriage. The Pharisees came and asked Him, "Is it lawful for a man to divorce his wife?" testing Him. And He answered and said to them, "What did

Moses command you?" They said, "Moses permitted a man to write a certificate of divorce and to dismiss her." And Jesus answered and said to them, "Because of the hardness of your heart he wrote you this precept. 'But from the beginning of the creation, God made them male and female.' 'For this reason a man shall leave his father and mother and be joined to his wife and the two shall become one flesh;' so then they are no longer two, but one flesh. Therefore what God has joined together, let no man separate."

As far as protection from diseases like STD/HIV is concerned, Jesus offered a divine wisdom by saying "the two shall become one flesh." This implies monogamy, only one sex partner. Anytime what Jesus said is literally reversed in direction and the two married sex partners becoming two, three, four, and so on, the consequences of that many sex partners is STD/HIV, AIDS, hepatitis B, hepatitis C, and herpes infection for life and most likely suffering and early death from either HIV/AIDS, hepatitis B, or hepatitis C infection.

Apostle Paul repeated what Jesus said in Ephesians 5:31–33 and continues to say that husband should love the wife and the wife should respect the husband in marriage. Paul said, "For this reason a man shall leave his father and mother and be joined to his wife, and the two shall became one flesh." This is a great mystery, but I speak concerning Christ and the Church. Nevertheless let each one of you in particular so love his own wife as himself and let the wife see that she respects her husband.

It is very important for married couples to openly discuss when to have sex especially when the woman is pregnant and even when there is misunderstanding. They should try not to stop having sex for a long time because many husbands and many wives have drifted away from being one flesh in marriage at a time of pregnancy and in times of simple misunderstanding or disagreements and got into having sex outside the marriage. This sexual behavior can lead to STD/HIV and its complications and sometimes infection of their babies with HIV.

The Jewish and Christian God has a lot of good information to help us prevent and control HIV epidemic. Therefore, believers of God must be more careful with their sex life and then step up and continue to teach such good news to prevent HIV infection and help to preserve marriages. The information will be beneficial to those who will consistently put the advice into practice and avoid getting and spreading HIV. A lot of people may not know that such deeper revelations about our sexual life are safety nets and provisions made by God to prevent us from suffering from chaos, dangers of life, and diseases.

I have found from STD/HIV field investigations that STD/HIV can affect both Christians and non-Christians who do not take these and many other Bible quotations about our sex life seriously enough to practice them. From the previous quotations and for many other similar predictions about our sexual lifestyle in the Bible, it is time to take the advice from the Bible seriously and adopt a healthy sexual lifestyle to reduce HIV epidemic until a cure is found.

Faith-based initiative to prevent STD/HIV will definitely work for those who believe in God and obey and practice what has been revealed through the Bible by the divine power of God about our sexual life. **A**bstinence, **Be** faithful to one sex partner (i.e., monogamy) and protecting other people from infectious disease has its roots in the Bible. Indeed those who believe in God and practice faith-based sexual behavior and test their would-be marriage partners for HIV before marriage will avoid HIV infection and a widespread consistent practice of such faith-based Biblical sexual behavior will help to limit the spread of HIV infection.

6

Behaviors, cultural practices, and beliefs affecting the STD/HIV epidemic

Some behaviors, cultural practices, and beliefs in communities, countries, and geographic regions of the world make it easier for people of certain genders, age groups, and personality traits to get STD/HIV than others. Transcultural practices due to easy communication by Internet and quick travel around the world can allow people to travel easily from one place to another and get infection with STD/HIV or spread STD/HIV.

Sexual behaviors of men and women

In the Western part of the world, especially in the United States and Europe, most HIV/AIDS cases have been found in men who have sex with men (MSM), men who have sex with both men and women (bisexuals), intravenous drug users, and those who abuse drugs (for example, cocaine, alcohol, marijuana), prison inmates and those who have a history of being incarcerated in jail or prison, people with a history of many sex partners, and people whose medical history includes STDs such as chlamydia, gonorrhea, and syphilis and their sex partners. Therefore most HIV/AIDS infections have been diagnosed in men even after twenty-five years of the HIV/AIDS epidemic despite the fact that women receive and retain most of the genital secretions from both men and women at the time of a sexual relationship.

Men, who decide to have sex without commitment to only one sex partner, have the opportunity to properly put on condoms to protect themselves and the sex partner, but most men do not use condoms or refuse to use them. Some men who have HIV infection do not care enough to protect their sex partner even when they know that they have HIV and have passed on HIV infection to other men (CDC 2006).

Men also have a better opportunity to protect themselves with condoms than women when they decide to have sex with a woman who is not their wife, but most men who are not committed to only one female sex partner and especially most men who never want to commit to any woman fail to use condoms and infect women with STD/HIV. Some men are having sex with men—a behavior that leads to more bruising and a likelihood of bleeding and contact with HIV in the blood and semen of an HIV positive sex partner. Besides, with anal sex, human sperm DNA is put into a stool medium of high growth of bacteria and viruses. Nobody knows and nobody can predict what will happen to the sperm DNA, which, unlike other human DNA, has been programmed by nature to produce a living organism. Bisexual men like person B in diagram 1 of chapter two are hiding their true identity from women and transmit HIV from high risk MSM sex partners to women.

Most women who decide to have sex with men outside marriage are failing to negotiate for commitment and get committed to only one man. Also such women are failing to negotiate for condom use. Women may be protected with male and female condoms as a way of staying healthy and alive to live a longer and healthy life free of HIV infection and take care of their children.

A lot of women are making decisions to have sex with men who have high-risk behaviors that make it easier to get HIV infection either knowingly or unknowingly without negotiating to agree for both of them to do a test for STD/HIV first at the beginning and then six months after starting a friendship with a man. They simply ignore doing it or have no money or means of access to an STD/HIV testing site and do not act to get HIV test done before committing to a sexual relationship. Some women also fail to consistently use condoms when they make decisions to have sex with someone who is not a married partner. This is a big mistake in the setting of the HIV/AIDS epidemic for a disease that has no cure.

I feel the pain of many such HIV positive women I have met in the course of my work in the hospitals, clinics, and public health departments for the past fourteen years. Women made the mistake of trusting men who didn't care about them. A lot of women have made mistakes by not protecting themselves and got HIV infection from men. They are dying from HIV/AIDS, leaving behind their orphan babies and children especially in the low-income African American and Hispanic populations in the U.S. and in Africa and developing countries.

Do not forget that testing together with a would-be sex partner for HIV and other STDs like gonorrhea, syphilis, chlamydia, and hepatitis B and C before a commitment to sex is a real demonstration of true love, caring, and responsibility to take care of each other. The truth is that nobody wants the person he or she loves to get sick from diseases especially from a disease that has no cure like HIV/AIDS. Looking at and confirming the test results to make sure that your would-be sex partner is HIV negative is one of the best decisions you can make for your life if you are the kind of person who does not want to get sick from a disease that can be prevented.

Take action to make the needed important decisions as an act of love. It is not a matter of trusting a person you just met. You don't know the previous sex life of this person, and you don't know who the person had sex with before you met. It is a matter of taking a responsibility to take care of each other and show that you truly love the person by modifying your sex life to take care of the person, and that begins by showing that you do not want to pass STD/HIV infection to that person.

Cultural practices and the HIV/AIDS epidemic in Africa and developing countries

Unlike the Western world where more men than women have HIV/AIDS, women have more HIV/AIDS infection than men in Africa and in most developing countries because the transmission of HIV infection is mainly by heterosexual relationships. This has happened because the men tend to have multiple female sex partners as part of a very old culture. The traditional marriages allow men to have many wives (polygamy) if they want. Such cultural practices and beliefs allow men to have many other female sex partners (concubines) if they have enough money or even little money or gifts to give to ladies and gifts for the would-be fathers- and mothers-in-law. Unfortunately, married men and wealthy men tend to have many additional wives and other female sex partners (girlfriends) that are several years younger than they are.

In Africa and the developing countries, younger and attractive girls 15–19 years old have more risk of entering into a sexual relationship with men many years older than them, who already have wives or many other uncommitted female sex partners. Such older men are likely to spread HIV infection to the younger female sex partners. It has been found in some African countries such as Ghana in West Africa, that though the HIV prevalence rate of 2.3% by 2005 was among the lowest in Africa, a cumulative database of newly diagnosed HIV/AIDS over a twelve-year period of HIV epidemic from 1986–1997 revealed that HIV incidence rate peaks five years earlier in females aged 25–29 than in males 30–34 years old. Incidence rate of HIV/AIDS in young females is higher than males, especially in the age group 15–19 years. The incidence is more than six times higher. Young females have a higher risk of getting HIV/AIDS than males, approximately 800 percent excess risk (Tabi and Frimpong 2003). In other words, the chance of young female getting HIV/AIDS is about eight times higher than young male in age group 15-19 years.

In some regions of the country, the female travelers to neighboring African countries especially Cote d'Ivoire are more likely to be HIV/AIDS positive and might have contributed to high numbers of HIV/AIDS for the period of 1986–1997 (Tabi and Frimpong 2003). A similar finding of higher HIV among young females 13–24 years old and male sex partners on average five years older than females have been described in South Africa (MacPhail 2002).

There are anecdotal reports that the men in Africa and developing countries entice these young women with promises of buying clothes, paying school fees, going on vacations, spending money, and buying many other gifts. Such men are called "sugar daddies" and are promiscuous and polygamous men. Therefore, the younger females have higher risk of having sex with them and getting HIV infection. Such unfortunate young females and female travelers and prostitutes develop AIDS by age 20–29 and die leaving behind many orphan babies and children (Tabi and Frimpong 2003).

By the process of vertical transmission, about 25 percent to 35 percent of those babies and children whose parents have higher risk of getting STD/HIV may have gotten the HIV/AIDS infection from their mothers at time of birth or through breastfeeding because no diagnosis was made at the time of pregnancy or at the time of birth to enable both the mother and the child to benefit from HIV medical treatment. In some African countries like Botswana, Zimbabwe, Lesotho, and Swaziland, approximately 23 percent to 35 percent of adults in reproductive ages 15–49 are living with HIV/AIDS infection, and more women have HIV/AIDS (World Development Indicators Database 2000).

The total fertility rate (the number of live babies born per thousand women age 15–45) is very high ranging from 3.6 to 6.4 in most African countries as noted by analysis of the sample fertility rate of sixteen countries in Africa with available fertility data that revealed seven out of the sixteen countries to have a fertility rate of 6.0 to 6.4 (Tabi and Frimpong 2003). In a setting of high birth rate, a high percentage of adolescents and adults 15–49 years old living with HIV/AIDS and then more young women getting HIV/AIDS, there is higher chance of more babies and infants getting HIV infection. HIV infection of newborn babies and infants could continuously worsen if more effective preventive measures such as prevention and treatment of HIV pregnant women and their babies as well as exclusive formula feeding of babies of HIV positive mothers are not made available, accessible, and affordable in Africa and developing countries. Such measures would prevent vertical transmission of HIV infection from mother to child at birth and by breastfeeding.

Role of policymakers: HIV infection of women and infants in Africa

Policymakers all around the world should take into consideration the behaviors and cultural practices just described when making decisions about the health of communities, counties, districts, regions, and nations they govern. These STD/HIV high-risk behaviors lead to HIV infection and disability, which indirectly decrease the labor force of the community and nations and make more people dependent on government resources. The gross domestic product (GDP, the market value of goods) of nations could be affected when the vibrant, energetic, and intellectual capacity of young adults is severely affected by HIV/AIDS.

Though people have the freedom to choose whatever sexual behavior they like, there are consequences and suffering associated with behaviors that deviate from the norm and more so when a behavior is associated with an infectious disease like HIV/AIDS. In spite of these facts, a lot of people will risk their lives and get infectious diseases that have no cure instead of modifying what they do and protecting themselves.

When there is an epidemic of infectious disease like HIV, behaviors that help the disease to spread from person to person is a concern for the community since everyone and especially the government, community leaders, and families have the responsibility to take care of the expenses of the sick person as well as the children who are affected directly and indirectly by the disease epidemic.

Adults stubbornly continue to do what they want even when it involves killing other people slowly with infectious disease that has no cure like HIV/AIDS, and children may suffer the consequences of these behaviors. What should policymakers do to protect children who are at risk of getting HIV infection at the time of birth and from breastfeeding?

The governments, health ministers, heads of local health departments, heads of divisions of infectious diseases control of STD/ HIV, physicians, nurses, and leaders of public health organizations including NGO and CBO must team up and mandate a clear policy for STD and HIV prevention and control. A policy should include primary prevention to reduce the number of people who will come into contact with STD/HIV per year. Groups need to develop innovative, effective behavioral interventions to educate new HIV positive patients to understand the HIV/AIDS disease process. Patients need to be encouraged to adhere to treatment plans and provide information for sex partner contacts. They need to be tested for early diagnosis and linkage to mental health, housing, drug rehabilitation, rehabilitation from sex for money and drugs to jobs for those who want such transitions. And most importantly, a policy that gives sex partners of known cases of HIV patients a chance to know that they have been exposed to HIV and offers them a rapid test such as OraQuick Advance Rapid HIV-1/2 Antibody test or OraSure will be essential to prevent them from unknowingly spreading HIV to other sex partners.

A team of well-trained disease intervention specialists (DIS) for STD/HIV can work with physicians at the HIV clinics and enroll HIV positive patients who are having unprotected sex and those infected with new STDs such as syphilis, chlamydia, and gonorrhea into effective HIV risk reduction behavioral interventions and confidential sex partner notification along with providing rapid HIV testing services to their sex partners. Such an active surveillance approach will help to find those who have high probability of getting HIV infections quicker and get them tested and linked to HIV medical care in case they test positive for HIV before they unknowingly transmit HIV infection to other people.

Late diagnosis of HIV/AIDS is unpleasant. This type of human suffering is preventable, and any policy implemented by policymakers and health care teams will need to work with those known to be living with HIV to prevent them from spreading the infection. If we do not continue to find out with whom a known HIV patient is having protected and unprotected sex with whenever they see a physician, we will fail to control the spread of HIV infection. HIV positive patients continue to have sex after being aware that they have HIV infection, and their sex partners must be given the chance to know of their HIV exposure so that they can modify what they do early.

It is not uncommon to find out that some of the sex partners of a known HIV-infected person have not yet gotten the infection at the time of confidential sex partner contact investigation and testing. Therefore, early notification of sex partners may help a lot of people to change or modify their sex life to prevent HIV infection. Otherwise, what you tend to see are people who test negative for HIV infection and within six months to a year or two years they test positive for HIV infection. It is quite sad to find that some of such cases occur after being in the same sexual relationship and others within a year or two after marriage. Most of them missed the chance to know of their HIV exposure and change or modify what they were doing or to stop a risky sexual relationship early enough to avoid HIV infection.

Some of the people who do regular testing every six months to a year or test for HIV before marriage were lucky to find that their sex partner was positive and they were negative. In such a case, those who decided to continue the sexual relationship with a known HIV positive person got the chance to use condoms consistently to protect themselves. This scenario has been found many times among heterosexual couples and has helped to prevent some of the HIV positive mothers whose husbands are HIV negative from infecting their husbands and babies. Besides, they have supportive husbands who are healthy to help support them and keep them healthy at the time they needed someone to help them cope with HIV/AIDS.

HIV/AIDS policies must mandate testing for HIV before marriage so that people are not deceived by those who know that they are HIV positive but failed to tell their would-be sex partners before marriage.

HIV infection is a chronic disease; therefore, anyone who has it will continue to be a source of spread until death as long as the person continues to be sexually active or inject drugs and share needles and syringes with other people. If we only elicit the sex partners' notification the first time a new HIV diagnosis is made, then we are not doing enough active surveillance to stay ahead of the spread of HIV infection.

A clear policy is needed for passive surveillance by people coming to health clinics, hospitals, and community testing centers to test for HIV infection. Also needed is active surveillance by continuous confidential sex partner notification of known new and old cases of HIV patients for the lifetime of each infected person, early linkage to HIV treatment and other supportive medical care, and effective behavioral intervention to decrease the spread of HIV infection to effectively prevent and control the HIV/AIDS pandemic.

The entire community and the governments especially in Africa and developing countries must help men to show more compassion for women and children and modify their behaviors to protect women and infants from HIV/AIDS. Women have a similar responsibility to think about protecting their babies from HIV/AIDS and to help men to protect themselves and the babies. The fact that men are the driving force for HIV/AIDS epidemics has been discussed. And the fact that women and children need more protection is vital. The families around the world especially in African countries as well as women's groups and movements and governments, churches, and community-based organizations and non-governmental organizations, doctors, nurses, and public health officials who are involved in policy making must take the HIV epidemic and sexual risk modification by citizens very seriously and help the process by mentoring and protecting young women and babies from HIV infection.

Some of the norms and cultures contributing to HIV/AIDS infection in women and children that need to be taken into consideration by policymakers are summarized here:

1. Early marriage of young girls to men several years older

2. Polygamous marriage

3. Lack of knowledge and ignorance about HIV/AIDS and STDs

4. Lack of ability of women to negotiate for sex and condom use by women

5. Economic dependency of women on men who may have other sex partners

6. Cultural norms and values that encourage reproduction in the setting of polygamy

7. Child bearing very important in marriage in the setting of polygamy

When an HIV positive woman is found to be pregnant, the following factors increase the chance of her passing the HIV infection to the baby: the cultural norms and practices, increased HIV viral load in the body, low CD4+ cell count, breastfeeding, and vaginal secretions (Tabi and Frimpong 2003).

Let us look at some of the limitations to protecting babies whose mothers have HIV infection at the time of pregnancy and breastfeeding in Africa and developing countries.

What Works	Limitations in Africa and Developing Countries
1. HIV medications given to pregnant women	1. Not readily available, expensive, shortage of qualified doctors, nurses and lab personnel and traditional healers (Tabi and Frimpong 2003)
2. HIV medication zidovudine and/or nevirapine given to mother and baby at birth and caesarian section	2. Not readily available, expensive, shortage of qualified doctors, nurses, lab personnel, and traditional healers
3. STD/HIV counseling and testing: "ABC," client and group specific risk, attitude norms, practices, and belief modifications	3. "ABC" done, testing and condom not affordable, and cultural beliefs leads to low condom use, and polygamy
4. No breastfeeding by HIV (+) mothers and exclusive formula feeding	4. Lack of money for formula feeding, milk and milk products and potable clean water for formula feeding
5. Education and economic empowerment	5. Economic dependency of women, sugar daddies, prostitution
6. Social support by family members	6. Stigmatization and secrecy barriers for medical care and family support
7. HIV/AIDS research	7. Lack of funding, data not analyzed to reflect group specific risk by local health departments

Every one of us who cares about babies has the responsibility to protect babies from diseases especially diseases that babies can get because of the parents' sexual behavior. One of the best things that can be done for babies to protect them from STD/HIV will be open discussion with a would-be sex partner and testing for STD/HIV and verifying each others' results before starting a sexual relationship and then follow-up HIV testing during the period of pregnancy and at time of delivery, whether it is a planned pregnancy or not. It is important to do everything possible to give every child the chance to be born without infectious diseases like HIV/AIDS that have no cure. Let us give these unborn babies a healthy beginning at the genesis of their life.

If an HIV positive woman is also pregnant, she is encouraged to do her best to begin taking medications for HIV to prevent AIDS as directed by the doctor and comply with the treatment. She should make sure to get treatment for HIV at the time of delivery of the baby. It is important that the baby is also given HIV medication at the time of birth and for a period of time ranging from one week to fourteen weeks as determined by the doctor.

The breast milk of HIV positive mothers has a 14 percent chance of infecting a baby. In case the mother and the baby do not get medication and the baby gets breastfeeding from the mother, there is 30 percent to 35 percent chance (that's one in three) that the baby will get HIV infection. Even if HIV medication is given to both the mother and the baby and then the mother breastfeeds, there is still a 14 percent chance that the baby will get HIV infection from the breast milk. The longer the mother breastfeeds the baby, the higher the chance she will pass on the HIV infection to the baby.

The HIV positive mother is encouraged to seek help from the family, the public health department, non-governmental organizations,

(NGOs), community-based organizations (CBOs), clinics, hospitals, and the government of the district, region, or the country to get formula feeding for the baby to protect the baby from HIV/AIDS and unnecessary suffering.

If the mother of a newborn baby lives in Africa or a developing country where formula feeding with milk and milk products is usually expensive, not available, or not feasible because of lack of potable clean water, she should be encouraged to seek help and get formula feeding for the baby. HIV positive women from poor countries are encouraged not to breastfeed their babies unless the mother and baby at the time of birth are both infected with HIV. A study in Zambia found that when the baby is already HIV infected by four months after birth and the baby does not get breastfeeding, there is a higher chance that the baby will die from complications of HIV/AIDS by twenty-four months after birth (Kuhn 2008).

Research has revealed that extended treatment of a baby whose mother has HIV infection with nevirapine for fourteen weeks appears to be safe (Kumwenda 2008). Treatment may be a better option when combined with exclusive formula feeding of the baby until the baby is weaned from formula feeds to traditional foods. It may be the best option for now to protect babies whose mothers have HIV infection from getting infected with HIV.

Government and public health policymakers in Africa and developing countries are encouraged to team up with community leaders, non governmental organizations (NGOs), community based organizations (CBOs), public health departments, hospitals clinics and other stakeholders to initiate policies and programs that give pregnant HIV positive mothers the opportunity to get HIV medications and continuous formula feeding for their babies after delivery at a very little or no cost at all. Policymakers all over the world are encouraged to initiate bold programs that will help people to modify their sexual lifestyles to avoid contracting HIV/AIDS and to protect babies from HIV/AIDS and continuously help governments in Africa to be more accountable for the welfare of their citizens such as the formula feeding of babies of all HIV positive mothers.

When governments in Africa run a country as if it were their personal property and do not invest in the talents of the people and build infrastructures to sustain their economies, the end result is poverty, less education, fewer jobs, hunger, childhood malnutrition, and death from childhood infectious diseases. Such a political climate also breeds fear, anger, political instability, professional and non-professional prostitution of men and women having multiple sex partners for money and infecting each other with STD/HIV infection.

In June 2008, I was taking my dear pregnant wife to the prenatal clinic when I heard on the radio that an NGO in South Africa called the Promise House was making an appeal for funds to raise enough money to support a project in Durbin that provides a home for abandoned babies of HIV positive mothers. Some of those children are HIV positive too, and the NGO needed money to buy drugs and food for the children.

I could not hold back my tears. I was weeping as I drove my wife to the clinic. I told myself that if my wife and I have been able to protect each other and give our baby the chance to be born without STD/HIV, our child is fortunate indeed to start life without infectious STD/HIV.

I wept also about the fact that for a period four or more years the government of South Africa had denied the potency of current

HAART to treat HIV and prevent patients from progressing fast to the end stage of AIDS and its complications. The former president Thabo Mbeki did not pursue aggressive treatment of HIV and HIV risk behavior intervention, and therefore the epidemic of HIV in South Africa has worsened, and more women are getting HIV infections. Therefore, vertical transmission of HIV from pregnant women to their babies increased. South Africa is not a poor nation compared to many African countries, yet it lacked the political will to prevent and control a scientifically proven HIV epidemic and to use the potency of HAART to slow down the progression of HIV to AIDS and also to prevent the vertical transmission of HIV infection from pregnant mothers to their babies.

The following articles appeared in the daily news of HIV/AIDS at CDC website.

The sources are cited as done by CDC. These are summerized examples of how the work and decisions by government and policymakers can impact HIV epidemic.

SOUTH AFRICA: South Africa to Draw a Line Under Years of Denial About HIV/AIDS

Source: Fri, 03 Oct 2008 - http://www.guardian.co.uk

Summary: According to this article, hundreds of thousands of South Africans have died of AIDS-related causes since 1999, and 5.5 million people are living with HIV/AIDS in the country. The new South Africa

President, Kgalema Motlante, appointed a new Health Minister, Barbara Hogan. She is quoted to have said that she is going to "get things right" by treating the country's HIV/AIDS epidemic seriously after years of gross government neglect. The article noted that the former President Thabo Mbeki who ruled from 1999 to September 2008, was condemned for making comments suggesting that HIV is not the cause of AIDS. He and the former Health Minister Manto Tshabalala-Msimang were criticized for delaying the implementation of AIDS treatment program when HIV medications became affordable in 2002. The former health minister is said to have encouraged the use of garlic, lemon and beets as treatment for the disease. The new health minister, Barbara Hogan, promised to avoid "cheap solutions" and "political games." "It is critically important that those who need treatment are able to get it." "We will as a matter of urgency examine all gaps in delivery."

Comment: The lack of political will to confront the HIV epidemic and use the intellectual talents of the country and community mobilization to control HIV infection can be devastating as revealed by the South African news article. The new South African government has demonstrated political will and leadership to care for the welfare and health of its citizens and control HIV/AIDS epidemic. Many more African leaders and governments in developing countries must learn from the South African HIV/AIDS prevention and control experience.

SOUTH AFRICA: South Africa Health Care Receives a Huge Cash Injection

Source: Wed, 22 Oct 2008 - http://www.bday.co.za

Summary: The policymakers in the new South Africa government have continued to demonstrate political will to control HIV epidemic. This article revealed that,the Finance Minister Trevor Manuel allocated extra money for dealing with the HIV/AIDS epidemic and plan to focus on long-term efforts to improve health infrastructure and retain skilled staff in the public sector. He allocated additional 300 million rand (US $28.6 million) for the cost of changing from using nevirapine-based mother-to-child HIV prevention to AZT-nevirapine treatment. The treasury director for health policy, Mark Bletcher was quoted as saying that the government's free HIV treatment program began in 2004 and since then, more than 500,000 HIV patients have started HIV medications, 200,000 of them in the last year. In 2008-09, an additional 1 billion rand (US $95.5 million) was made available for occupation-specific wage dispensation for nurses, and will be expanded to other categories of health care workers, such as doctors and pharmacists,by the next three years to help retain staff in the public health. Additional 30,000 public health workers have been employed within the last three years.

Comment: It is very important for government and health departments all over the world to support the training of more doctors, nurses, pharmacist, laboratory sciences and public health workers to work in a coordinated team effort to control HIV epidemic. In 2007, an estimated 2 million people died from AIDS and 2.7 million contracted the virus. Currently, infected patients can benefit from HAART that effectively delay or prevent progression to AIDS (Palella FJ Jr, New England Journal of Medicine 1998).

Millions of new HIV/AIDS patients, usually young adults, have been added to the disease pool of patients in many countries because of HIV infection but more health care workers have not been trained to control the epidemic. South Africa's effort is commendable and many countries that are in denial of the need of more health care workers must learn from South Africa's example. Since HIV is a chronic disease and people will live with it for a longer period on medications, it is urgent that we train more medical staffs to meet the current demand especially in the area of doctors and nurses, mental health and HIV disease investigation epidemiologist and intervention specialist to provide effective and efficient support system for known HIV positive persons and help protect the community from the spread of HIV/ AIDS.

Economic hardships among minority populations have led to a process whereby men who have some money want to have multiple female sex partners, and some women want to have as many male sex partners as possible to survive the economic hardship of unemployment. High-risk sexual and drug-seeking behavior for money especially amongst minority populations in the world, have contributed to many people making mistakes and contracting STD/HIV. Black African American women and women in developing countries especially Africa, continue to have increasing numbers of HIV infection because of dependent behavior on men in the setting of economic hardships. Many of such men have many other girlfriends, and in some places in the world, some of such men have sex with other men and transmit HIV infection to women.

For instance, the United Nations Program on HIV/AIDS reported in the UNAIDS fact sheet 2004 that 1.8 million adults and children in Zimbabwe are living with HIV/AIDS. Twenty four percent (24.6%) of adults (15-46 years) in Zimbabwe are HIV positive: the fourth prevalence highest rate in the world and women represent fifty eight percent (58%) of HIV positive adults (15-49 years). Approximately 64.2% of Zimbabweans live on less than two US dollars a day ($2/day) and 34.9% are living under the national poverty line. Girls and young women make up nearly eighty percent (80%) of young people between the ages of 15-24, living with HIV/AIDS. The report says that a key factor driving HIV infection amongst girls and young women is intergenerational sex. Nearly a quarter of women in their twenties are in relationship with men 10 years older than them. (UNAIDS, 2004). Experts fear that widespread unemployment is causing the nation's young people to fall into despair and engage in high-risk activities.

Zimbabwe, like many other African countries, has gone through a period of political instability and less accountability to the people that the government is elected to serve. The results of poor government and political instability have caused a great deal of brain drain to European countries and North America, poverty and unsafe sexual behaviors, and an HIV/AIDS epidemic. A political will to initiate bold safe sex behavior models is essential for Africa to protect women and children from HIV/AIDS.

Comply with HIV treatment and STD/HIV health education and reduce stigma

There is treatment for HIV infection but no cure. People who know that they have HIV infection in the early stages of the disease, by testing and then following up consistently with their physicians for treatment and monitoring of their CD4 and viral load to keep the CD4 count within the normal range and HIV viral undetectable, are living longer. The process of compliance to follow up with the physicians helps them to decide when to start HIV medications. Check the summaries of the CDC HIV/AIDS news story that follows about HIV treatment:

UNITED STATES: HIV Doctors May Treat All Infected, Adding Thousands

Source: Wed, 29 Oct 2008 - http://www.bloomberg.com

Summary: According to this article, scientist at the 48th Annual Interscience Conference on antimicrobial agents and chemotherapy in Washington discussed the fact that starting HIV treatment at CD4 count of 500 would save lives instead of waiting for CD4 count to reduce to 350 before treatment. Normal CD4 count is 600-1200. Paul Sax, a Havard Medical School AIDS expert who helped to write the current guidelines is quoted as saying that "We may be heading for a time when all patients are benefiting from HIV treatment. It is noted that heart diseases and cancer are more common among HIV patients with high CD4 count who have not been started on HIV treatment.

The report mentioned a research finding which suggested

that HIV patients who have undetectable viral loads because they are taking medications for HIV are less likely to transmit HIV. The director of National Institute of Allergy and Infectious Diseases, Anthony Fauci, is quoted as saying that "the new data seem to indicate that there is an advantage to starting earlier." These scientists have concerns about the HIV medication side effects and emerging of drug-resistant virus that can develop when HIV medication regimens are not closely monitored. The US Department of Health and Human Services and the International AIDS Society recommends that HIV positive patients who have no symptoms should start HIV medication treatment when their CD4 counts fall to 350.

Comment: Universal yearly testing of people with low risk behavior for STD/HIV and six monthly testing of STD/HIV of people with high risk behavior must be encouraged because it is better to know STD/HIV results early and benefit from treatment. Persons who were diagnosed with HIV early and continuously followed up with their doctors every three months and then started HAART medications for HIV early at the time they needed medications to reduce the HIV viral load to undetectable level and kept their CD4 count above 500/ul are living longer than persons who do not test early and were diagnosed late with HIV and AIDS. Persons diagnosed late with HIV/AIDS suffer from more complications. Early detection of HIV infection by testing and early treatment will be beneficial and may help control HIV epidemic especially if the sex partners are given the chance to be confidentially informed, tested and treated for HIV infection early before they unknowingly spread it.

Prophylactic treatment for sexual exposure to HIV have not been actively pursued by physicians because of the concern that HIV may become resistant to the medications. Perhaps, a prophylactic treatment for sex partners of a known HIV positive persons within the past one year who initially test negative for HIV may help prevent sex partners from developing HIV infection later in case they are in the window period of HIV infection. Such a prophylactic treatment for HIV may then be stopped when the second follow up test for HIV in three to six months is negative. The sex partners whose second test turn positive will then continue to take the HAART for HIV as a form of early treatment for Universal treatment of HIV infection.

All locatable sex partners to STDs are given prophylactic treatment for the specific STDs involved until results of the STD test is known. May be we need to do the same for sex partners of known HIV positive persons until the results of the second HIV test results is known. As at now, we have not tried a universal prophylactic treatment of HIV for sexual contact over a longer period because of concerns of development of HIV resistance to the medication, HAART, for the treatment and control HIV/AIDS. Further research about prophylactic treatment for HIV must be pursued and the benefit and cost-effectiveness of such prevention compared to the living with HIV for a lifetime on HAART assessed before it could be implemented.

However, medical research has found out that such post-exposure prophylaxis for HIV is effective when given within 72 hours of occupational exposure (accidental needle puncture of health workers involved in patient care) and non-occupational exposure (rape victims and sex partners of a known HIV positive person) to HIV. An example of HIV medication for post-exposure prophylaxis is combivir.

Compliance to take all the daily dosage of combivir for a period of 28 days is recommended by CDC, and it is necessary to prevent

HIV infection at a cost of $785.00. The person should be seen and monitored for combivir side effects and compliance with treatment by a physician.

Post-exposure prophylaxis for HIV is an effective prevention method to protect a baby from vertical transmission of HIV from HIV positive mother during the period of pregnancy, birth and after birth and it is widely implemented. Post-exposure prophylaxis or vaccination of sex partners who unknowingly had unprotected sex with a confirmed HIV positive partner, needs more public health attention and research.

There is no pre-exposure prophylaxis or vaccination for HIV infection now, until medical research suggest that it is efficient and cost-effective.

Many HIV patients are living longer on HIV medications, good nutrition, safe sex practice with only one sex partner, and use of condoms to prevent STDs like syphilis, which can quickly spread to the brain of HIV patients. However, there are some known HIV patients who continue to spread HIV infection and in the process acquire other STDs like syphilis, gonorrhea, chlamydia, hepatitis B, hepatitis C, HPV, herpes simplex and trichomoniasis.

Those who have HIV infection and are protecting themselves and their sex partners by making them aware of their HIV positive results and complying with their treatment and living a healthy life must reach out to other HIV patients who have lost all hope and are depressed. Sharing the information that people can know their HIV positive status early and do the right things that will help them live and benefit from treatment and be positive about what they can do usually helps a newly diagnosed HIV patient to cope with the stress and depression associated with the diagnosis of HIV infection. They can also work as peer leaders for HIV-related behavior modification and help new HIV positive patients to understand how to live with HIV infection and adhere to HIV medical treatment, inform their sex partners of their HIV status, and consistently use condoms when they decide to have sex and do follow-up health maintenance care with a physician for the rest of their lives.

The families and communities must reach out to those who have HIV infection in a positive way, as they comply with treatment directives to do no harm to themselves and others. It is time to educate the present generation that people with HIV are living longer with diseases and need support since HIV is not spread by casual contact like talking, handshaking, sharing toilets, and living in the same house and the same environment once a person is not sexually involved with an HIV patient or not sharing needles and syringes for injection of drugs. There is absolutely no need for stigma because HIV does not spread by casual contact. HIV positive person should be assured of acceptance in the community and HIV positive person must try as much as possible not to use stigma as a reason not to disclose HIV status to a sex partner. We have evidence that HIV positive persons who tell their sex partners can remain in sexual relationship and keep the sex partner's HIV status negative by consistent use of condom (KIMBERLY AW, 2006). Disclosure of HIV positive status without stigma is a responsibility to protect, care and love by the community, sex partners and HIV positive persons.

Treatment for HIV has significantly been found to reduce the stigma associated with disclosure of HIV status. The following news articles from CDC HIV/AIDS daily news may be clues to step up mass media HIV education about treatment and living with HIV, to increase community awareness, and to help people living with HIV gain more acceptance and support in the community. The families and the communities must support a process that will make testing for HIV every six months to a year a norm for every sexually active person who has not limited sex to one partner as exemplified by a faithful marriage relationship, every person prior to marriage, women especially African American women, and men who depend on many male sexual partners for money in exchange for sex and drugs either as a prostitute with many sex partners (knowingly a prostitute or not), young men who have left their homes and depend on other men for money or drugs in exchange for sex, men who have multiple female sex partners, those who inject drugs, and those who have sex with anonymous sex partners such as people they meet on the Internet. All such people with high risk of HIV need help, and those ready to change need support to make behavioral changes.

A process that will facilitate and recognize HIV positive disclosure to a sex partner and families, testing and treatment of HIV as a protective behavior needs to be encouraged by society as a norm since HIV patients are living longer now and must be encouraged to adopt safe behaviors that do not lead to the spread of HIV infection.

Families must not abandoned HIV patients who adopt safe behaviors. They should integrate them as valuable community partners who can help others to understand the disease and protect others from getting HIV infection especially in young people between the ages of thirteen and twenty-four. Many young HIV patients are finding it difficult to relate to their families, especially young men who have sex with men. They lose hope in the setting of early diagnosis and good treatment for HIV infection.

Let us read the following news articles and limit the stigma associated with HIV infection. These articles from around the world have been added to stimulate discussion about STD/HIV infection.

A summarized report of CDC HIV/AIDS daily news from Africa:

BOTSWANA: The Impact of Universal Access to Antiretroviral Therapy on HIV Stigma in Botswana

Source: Mon, 01 Sep 2008 - http://www.apha.org/journal/AJPH2.htm

Summary: The article reported that Botswana initiated a National Universal HIV treatment program and after three years, a follow up research using a population based survey of one thousand two hundred and sixty eight adults (1268) in 2004 was done to find out about the impact of treatment access on HIV stigma. 38% of the participants reported at least one stigmatizing attitude, 23% would not purchase food from a shopkeeper with HIV, 5% would not care for an HIV-infected relative. 70% reported at least one measure of anticipated stigma, 54% anticipated ostracism after testing HIV positive and 31% anticipated mistreatment at work. Perceived access to HIV treatment was strongly and independently associated with decrease probability (i.e. the odds) of stigma attitude (adjusted odds ratio = 0.42; 95% confidence interval = 0.24-0.74) and of anticipated stigma (adjusted odds ratio = 0.09; 95% confidence interval = 0.03-0.30).

The finding is significant and suggest that access to HIV treatment may be a factor for reducing HIV stigma. The stigmatizing attitudes and anticipated stigma may persist which suggest that HIV stigma must be a target for ongoing intervention.

Comment: It is obvious from this report that many people (95%) would care for HIV-infected relatives. And also HIV positive persons may think of stigma from other people (70% anticipated stigma) more than it is necessary. Since HIV treatment strongly decrease stigma attitude, we need to encourage HIV positive persons to comply with treatment.

We must educate the community about the benefits of treatment and to accept HIV positive persons because the spread of HIV is to unprotected sex partners, needle and syringe sharing partners and not by casual contact such as talking to HIV positive person, hand shake, sharing the same plates, cups, toilet seats, office space and living together in the same house. We have a good blood screening test to detect HIV in donated blood before transfusion which reduces the chance of spreading HIV to many people in the community by blood donation.

The following are summarized report of CDC HIV/AIDS daily news articles from United States and sources as cited by CDC:

FLORIDA: Outreach Workers Battle AIDS Denial on St. Lucie Streets

Source: Thu, 25 Sep 2008 – http://www.tcpalm.com

Summary: From this report, St. Lucie County had the highest HIV rate in Florida for black women and the 6th highest for white women in 2007. The HIV prevention staff from the Image of Christ worked on the streets at night, offering condoms and free oral swab HIV screening to resident. There were anecdotal reports by the staff about denial, ignorance and refusal to talk about HIV and that could have contributed to the high rates of HIV in the County. Heterosexual women whose sex partners are men who have sex with men (MSM), a high incarceration of males and their need to survive in prison and then reclaim their manhood by going back to their girlfriends and their wives was cited by Dawn Jones, HIV/AIDS program coordinator, as partly explaining the high infection rate in the black women and black community. There were anecdotal reports that:

People think you can get HIV by sitting on toilet seat.

Teens think that only vaginal sex is sex and put themselves at greater risk by practicing anal sex.

Many teens are not practicing abstinence.

Comment: Denial, ignorance and misinformation about the means of spread of HIV infection should always be addressed in HIV prevention education. Bisexual men are very high risk group for the spread of HIV to women especially black women. Women must negotiate HIV testing with a would-be sex partner and verify test results even when the person is a former sex partner, and protect themselves from HIV. Women in general have more risk of getting STD/HIV from sex with a man who has HIV infection and men have more risk of getting HIV infection by having sex with men who have sex with men (also known as gays) because men who have sex with men have high rate of HIV than any other group.

Practising anal sex increases chance of getting HIV infection and all the other STD because there is more bruising and likelihood of bleeding by anal sex than any other forms of sex. This makes it easy for HIV and all other STDs to be transmitted by anal sex. Females and men should be told not to practice anal sex as a means of preventing pregnancy or STD/HIV because it increases the chance of getting HIV/AIDS infection which has no cure. Oral sex like any other sexual practice which allow genital secretions and fluids from one person to enter the other person can transmit STDs including HIV infection.

Abstinence is the best means of preventing contact with STD/HIV and must be encouraged in teens so that those who will listen and practice it can protect themselves from the troubles of STD/HIV infections and its financial burden. Those who do not want to live with HIV/AIDS in early period of their lifes and want to secure a better healthy lifestyle need to hear it and must be encouraged to practice it until they are ready as adults to make the right decisions about sex partners who will protect them from HIV/AIDS.

There is no scientific evidence of HIV infection from sitting on toilet seat and casual contact like handshake, kissing, hugging, drinking and eating from same items with HIV positive person. Talking and discussing STD/HIV prevention with sex partner and taking action to protect each other is essential to avoid getting HIV/AIDS and early death.

MICHIGAN: Young, Black, Gay and Vulnerable

Source: Wed, 24 Sep 2008 - http://www.freep.com/

Summary: From this report, the Michigan Department of Health noted that gay African American males aged 13-24 make up seventeen percent (17%) of the total HIV/AIDS cases in Detroit and the HIV rates has been rising in gays in that age group. In their efforts to prevent HIV, the CDC and AIDS Partnership Michigan have supported a Real Enough 2 Change (R.E.C) Boyz program that intergrates HIV prevention messages into various activities and home prevention parties where people can be screened for HIV. These are anecdotal reports from the outreach workers:

"This generation didn't live through the 80's when people were burying their friends."

"It is easy to be fooled into believing everything is okay."

"Plus, the fact that they're young and just coming out makes them more vulnerable."

"They have lost love of their family and friends."

"If they are living on the streets or couch-surfing, condoms are the last thing on their list."

"Many look for outward signs of HIV in a sex partner, unaware the infection can be asymptomatic."

"Superman Syndrome: "They know there's a danger, but they think they're made of steel."

According to the report, one of the outreach workers who is a known HIV positive said that "we want to change the norms of the whole community. Condoms aren't optional. They're necessary every time."

Comment: The above observation and efforts by these HIV outreach workers in Michigan reflects what is going on among young black men who have sex with men. The efforts of these workers and their reports needs to be taken serious by families and communities everywhere and help provide support for young black men before they get into situations that make them homeless and vulnerable to HIV infection. STDs and HIV are more common in homeless population. Denial and lack of knowledge of HIV risk and the spread from sex partners makes the youth and young black men more vulnerable to HIV especially when they are sexually active, change from having sex with women to sexual relationship of men with men and refuse to use condoms always.

UNITED STATES: CDC Says 1.1 Million Americans Infected with HIV

Source: Thu, 02 Oct 2008 - http://www.reuters.com and Morbidity and Mortality Weekly (MMWR) report 2008

Summary: This report estimated the existing rate (prevalence) of HIV to be 447.8 case per 100,000 population based on reports of new infections from 40 states with the best data, AIDS diagnoses and deaths from all 50 states, and extended back-calculation. This improved surveillance data used by CDC estimated that 994,000 people were living with HIV/AIDS in 2003. It noted that the number of people living with HIV is growing as more people become infected and as effective treatments delay AIDS-related deaths.

In this report, Richard Wolitski, the acting chief of CDC's HIV/AIDS prevention division is quoted as saying, "These data really show the continued impact that the epidemic is having on Americans, and they really reinforce the severe toll that is expected on multiple communities,"

The data revealed that African Americans and gay and bisexual men are disproportionally affected:

Males comprised 74.8 percent of prevalent HIV cases.

48.1 percent of all cases were attributed to male-to-male sexual contact.

High-risk heterosexual sex accounted for 27.6 percent of infections, including 72.4 percent of cases among women.

Injection drug use was the cause of 18.5 percent of HIV cases.

African Americans represented 46.1 percent of all people living with HIV in 2006 in Unites States.

In 2006, one in five Americans with HIV—232,700—did not know they were infected.

From the report, Wolitski said, "We're not going to be able to treat our way out of this epidemic." "We need to have strong prevention programs so we can prevent these infections from occurring in the first place."

Comment: It is obvious that people are living longer with HIV/AIDS on HIV medications. I agree with Richard Wolitski that we need strong prevention programs to prevent HIV. It is necessary to protect people from getting HIV infection from known previous HIV positive persons. Behavior modification models and interventions such as the CDC approved Diffusion of

Effective Behavior Interventions (DEBIs) have been used to control the spread of HIV to some extend but now that we know that HIV positive patients are living longer, it is time to combine more intensive epidemiologic HIV disease investigations with behavior interventions and work with HIV positive patients through risk assessments from their doctors office to STD/HIV public health field investigation workers and stop the spread of HIV by known HIV positive patients.

ALASKA: Some Alaska Students Seek More Sex Education

Source: Wed, 01 Oct 2008 - http://www.ap.org/

Summary: According to this report, in Anchorage, Alaska, some students were in the process of sending petition to the State of Alaska to teach comprehensive sex education in schools instead of leaving sexual health instruction to individual districts. The group known as Voices for Planned Parenthood (VOX) had collected list of names of one thousand and one hundred people supporting the petition through the Planned Parenthood to the State. Comments by some of the those sending the petition were as follows:

-Experience in School has been a motivation to seek a change at the State level.

-"I know exactly how bad the sex ed was because I sat through it too."

-"We were not informed."

-Alaska has a history of deferring a sex education.

-"Contraceptives is not part of our curriculum nor is it stressed or talked about. It's a very controversial issue in so many places because a lot of parents don't want the schools doing it all; other parents absolutely want the schools to do it. And then you've got a lot of people in between."

-Someone said she would consider attaching a sex education unit to high school health class. "At this point, there has not been an official request. I am more than willing to have the health curriculum committee look at this issue."

The report noted that Anchorage follows abstinence-plus model, which stresses abstinence as the only sure way to prevent STDs and pregnancy. Teachers provide instruction on what to do if students choose to have sex. Students learn about biology of reproduction in some Public Schools.

Comment: The term "sex education" is very confusing to many parents of school children who think that schools may be teaching their children how to have sex. We know that School Health Education is not planned to teach children how to have sex and that is not what the teachers teach the children.

We should stop confusing parents and tell them exactly what the school health education is about and stop using the term "sex education". Perhaps the part of school health that involves the teaching of reproductive health could be called developmental stages in adolescents and prevention of STD/HIV. That is exactly what it is supposed to teach and the meaning will be clear to parents.

The use of contraceptive could have adverse side effects on the body with the exception of condoms. Since condom use is mention as part of STD prevention, School children who request for contraception should be referred to public health departments and clinics or school clinic where a well trained staff and clinicians can assess the individual risk for using a particular type of contraceptive before recommending it to high school student.

Pregnancy is something that can start occurring at a certain developmental age in adolescents and young adults. Therefore, the prevention of teenage pregnancy can be discussed and the contraceptive aspect mention but children are made aware to talk to their school clinic nurse or clinician about the contraceptive options. Such arrangement would make parents more receptive to school health education which actually involves the teaching of basics of disease prevention and many health topics that will be beneficial to children and parents. We should not label school health as "sex education."

Schools should be encouraged to allow public health department personnel involved in STD and HIV disease investigation to share valuable STD/HIV prevention information with the children that will help them to make better choices before they are lured into sexual behaviors that have proven over years to cause serious health problems and may also affect the reproductive life of those who want to give birth to children in the future.

Parents usually do not object the process of sharing health information that will protect and prevent their children from getting STD/HIV infection.

FLORIDA: Reports Suggest that Socially Conservative Attitudes, Common in Southern Cities Such as Jacksonville, Make It More Difficult to Fight the Spread of AIDS

Tue, 30 Sep 2008 - http://www.jacksonville.com

Summary: According to this report, the Southern AIDS Coalition (SAC) cites "social conservatism" as one of the key reason why the Southern part of the United States leads the nation's four regions in the number of AIDS cases. The following anecdotal reports were noted:

"Shame and fear of stigmatizing reactions on the part of others may lead to reluctance to seek testing and treatment for HIV and other STDs."

"Anecdotal evidence across the South indicates that the prominence of the church, with its sexual prohibitions, intensifies fear of stigma."

The report said that homophobia and lack of awareness was discussed as part of cultural barriers to HIV/AIDS prevention at the International AIDS Conference 2008 in Mexico City and there was anecdotal report that such barriers exist in the Southern Cities of the United States and mentioned Jacksonville in Duval County as example thus;

In 1996, a lawsuit forced Duval County's sex education component to go from abstinence-only to include discussions of abstinence and birth control. Parents can exempt their children from the lessons, though only around one percent (1%) do so."

The State no longer funds billboards or bus signs as part of its public awareness campaign in Jacksonville.

"There is this underlying (sentiment of), 'We don't want this to be visible." Concluded the statements from the anecdotal reports.

Comment: Health workers including doctors, nurses and public health workers who test and help people with STDs and HIV positive results to get treatment and continuous medical care, have open policy to help the sick and the community to prevent and get treatment for diseases including STDs and HIV. There is treatment for HIV but no cure yet and therefore HIV medical providers wish that HIV positive persons will continuous comply with their follow up visits to the clinic to see their doctors and the supportive medical team and stay healthy and give their sex partners the chance to test for HIV and benefit from treatment and medical care.

Medical providers and the health workers want HIV positive persons and their sex partners to have better quality life before they get AIDS and suffer and die earlier than expected. They keep STD and HIV information about their patients confidential. Therefore, reluctant to test and seek treatment for HIV is unfortunate 'self-inflicted perceived stigma' which is not good for HIV positive persons and the community. Health workers want to see more people test and benefit from treatment and medical care for HIV and STDs before they suffer from complications of these diseases.

Stigmatization by itself, does not cause HIV spread because it cannot serve as a carrier of HIV. It is what we are doing to each other in our intimate sexual relationship by having multiple sex partners, not caring enough to protect each other and not tell our sex partners about a positive HIV status and hiding our true sexual life from our sex partners that is contributing to the spread of HIV infection and killing each other with HIV. And so the health department workers, doctors, nurses, political and community leaders and religious leaders must actively educate their communities to know and understand that HIV positive persons cannot spread HIV infection by casual contact and therefore deserve to be accepted and treated with dignity.

The community should openly accept mass communication to keep them informed and stay healthy and make testing for HIV and acceptance of HIV positive status a normal part of our health care to stay healthy. A healthy mind is found in a healthy body and a healthy community without HIV will make a healthy economy. The process of hiding a disease epidemic like HIV until it gets out of control is not good for the community.

It is common for known HIV positive persons to have a perceived stigmatization whereby HIV positive persons think that if they make people aware that they have HIV infection, people may not want to associate with them, family may not want to live with them, they may lose their friends, the church may not accept them and therefore they may not want anybody to know that they are HIV positive. What then tend to happen is that perceived stigma may not make HIV positive person disclose their HIV positive status to their sex partners because of fear of rejection and then make mistakes and infect their sex partners with HIV infection or acquire additional dangerous STD like Hepatitis B, C and syphilis by unprotected sex. We know a lot about HIV now and how people can get it and so mass education of the community is needed to reduce and stop perceived stigma and a stigma of any other forms about HIV infection.

For past centuries, the Church had shared and continues to share very important information with people and the community about human behaviors and consequences of behaviors that are self-destructive, prevention and healing of diseases. The information share by the church is based on historical facts with numerous eye witness accounts of accuracy of predicting the consequences of behaviors, has open message applicable to all people without discrimination of past behavior. What happens then is that once a person joins the church as a sign of belief in God, that person is expected to modify and change the old behavior which lead to diseases and problems and will lead to diseases in the future, suffering, death and self-destruction and could have negative impact on the community.

The church cannot be blamed for stigma because what the church says has historical and Biblical backing and has demonstrated in the past and present to support people who belief in its teachings and put them into practice to avoid diseases like leprosy, HIV and other STDs as well as the good Samaritan story that have been adopted and advanced by hospitals, clinic and doctors all over the world and have helped to save millions of lives in emergency situations like heart attack, stroke, injuries from vehicle accidents and fire and many other deadly situations. The Church supports spiritual healing and then physical treatment of HIV by clinics and hospitals. The church has supported homeless HIV positive clients and continue to feed and provide a place of residence for many of them in Jacksonville. There are many HIV positive persons who get their best of support from their pastors in Jacksonville. You should expect the church to continue to teach those good messages that help to preserve life, prevent suffering, save cost of medical care and give all people the chance to modify their behavior to prevent diseases and suffering.

We should not expect the teachings of the church about behavior issues to change. Imagine what will happen in the world without those behavior modifications and changes supported by the church. For instance, if a person has more than one sex partner that person and the sex partners have a chance of getting STD and HIV even if that person is a pastor of a church. And so by teaching that people should commit to only one sex partner in marriage and avoid sex before marriage, the church has given the community a very important disease prevention information. It is likely that not all people can consistently put that into practice but that should not prevent many people from hearing that message and always applying them to their lives.

Perceived stigma by known HIV positive persons make them think that the church will not accept them. On the contrary, the church is meant to bring healing do the sick, food to the poor, visit and help to those in prison and suffering, love of neighbors like we love our bodies and good information about behaviors changes that will help to prevent suffering now and the future. Indeed, many churches have support ministry for people living with HIV/AIDS and do not expect a person who is HIV positive to spread the disease to their neighbors and will therefore teach a change of behavior to protect, love and care for a neighbor.

CALIFORNIA: AIDS Walk More than a Fundraiser

Wed, 01 Oct 2008 - http://www.pe.com

Summary: The Inland Project in Fairmount Park in Riverside, California, was reported to be hosting its 18th annual AIDS Walk. There was anecdotal report that the annual AIDS walk is a "kind of pep rally to get people refocused on the importance of addressing AIDS in our community." "Since people are living longer with HIV, many people are assuming that AIDS has been addressed and is going away, and the actual truth is that the number of people who tested positive for HIV in Riverside and San Bernardino counties went up during a two-year period by 25 percent." (Reference:www.inlandaidsproject. org).

Comment: Community mobilization and engagement in discussion to increase the awareness of persistent threat of HIV/AIDS must be pursued continuously. Community leaders must use it as opportunity to engage public health workers, people affected by HIV/AIDS and people in the community in a team effort to modify HIV transmission behaviors and protect each other. Action plans need to be formulated and implemented in a manner similar to investigation and prevention of disease outbreak to reverse the trends of increasing number of HIV/AIDS and its impact on the health and well-being of the community.

Community support and acceptance of those affected by HIV/AIDS as they continue to live longer on HIV medications is always necessary to help them to modify their behavior and stop being a source of spread of HIV. They must be motivated to disclose their HIV positive status by informing and protecting their sex partners. Encouraging disclosure of HIV positive status and acceptance without stigmatization, testing for HIV and protection of sex partners must be pursued by communities to reduce the HIV/AIDS epidemic.

DISTRICT OF COLUMBIA: Elder Think Tank Offers HIV Discussion

Source : Thu, 02 Oct 2008 - http://www.metroweekly. com

Summary: The report mentioned that the Washington DC's gay community center had planned a seminar "HIV over 50" to help educate seniors about the continuing threat of AIDS as part of ongoing "Elder Think Tank" gathering. Two physicians were invited to discuss HIV/ AIDS treatment.

Comment: HIV/AIDS has significantly affected gay (in other words, MSM) community and bisexual males more than any other group. CDC data from 33 states in the United States showed that the number of HIV/AIDS cases increased among adult and adolescent MSM in all age group from 2001 to 2005. Black African American MSM ages 13-24 had the largest increase (source; HIV/AIDS News: www.medicalnewstoday.com/articles/100743.php).

The issues of numerous anonymous sex partners, easily available sex partners at clubs and bathhouses, from internet websites, chat-line and chat-rooms ready to have sex without disclosure of HIV status, without commitment and refusal to use condom to protect each other as evidenced by higher number of syphilis and HIV must be addressed. The group is not protecting each other as expected and what they are doing to each other are the main issues that needs to be discussed, confronted and resolved. If no efforts are made to protect each other, HIV and all the other STDs will continue to pose a serious health hazards to the gay community and bisexuals.

Recent emergence of increased sexual transmission of Hepatitis C

Samuel Frimpong MD, MPH

in gay men with history of HIV positive in London and continental European around 2002 and the fourty two percent (42%) increase in hepatitis C among HIV-positive men in University of California-San Francisco's (UCSF's) Positive Health Program is another wake up call for the need to be more careful and protect each other. Similar increase of co-infection of hepatitis C in known HIV positive persons have been found in New York (source: Thu, 26 Mar 2009, http://enbar. com). People must be made aware of the fact that a liver failure from hepatitis C will make it difficult for HIV medication to work because the process of detoxification of the medication by the liver will fail. Side effects of HIV medication must be expected to worsen in HIV patients who get hepatitis C and Hepatitis B infection and then liver failure.

Higher increase in syphilis in the gay (MSM) community than any other group has emerged in many large cities in United States since 2006 than early part of this decade. Many of those affected do not care if their sex partners get the chance to be treated with medications for syphilis and others have many anonymous sex partners especially from the internet, chat room and chat lines. This is a very serious issue that need to the discussed, sex partners notified and commitment to STD/HIV prevention plan taken serious to reduce the spread of STD/HIV in the MSM and the associated financial burden on the government and the community.

The bisexual males must make their female sex partners aware of their sex life. Failure to do so for any other reasons, pose a health hazard to females and then to babies who are born by mothers infected with HIV by bisexual men. Females should be proactive about verifying HIV test results of men before commitment to sex and protect themselves

216

from getting STD/HIV from bisexual men. Females who have sex with bisexual men have a higher chance of getting STD/HIV.

Young men and especially young black African American men who are choosing gay and bisexual lifestyle must be educated about the future health challenges especially the higher chance of getting HIV from sex partner and the consequences of living with HIV/AIDS. They have a higher chance of getting HIV infection than any other group in United States since 46% of black African American MSM are HIV positive. Many black MSM are bisexual and by hiding their true identity "down low" from black women, they continue to pose a major source of HIV infection to African American women. It is very common to find such young black MSM, depressed after contracting HIV infection, in denial of being HIV positive, confused about the impact of the disease and not regularly keeping their HIV clinic appointment. Many of them are diagnosed late with complications of AIDS and die earlier than other groups because of poverty and inability to afford balance nutrition, housing and mental health problems of depression and social isolation from families. The families of black MSM should do whatever they can to be supportive of behavior modification and medical care especially when there is a diagnosis of HIV infection.

Washington, DC's HIV epidemic has a prevalence rate of approximately three percent (3%) and is comparable in rates to some African Countries like Nigeria which had estimated adult HIV/AIDS prevalence rate of 3.1 percent in 2005 (source: USAID HIV/AIDS Country Profile for Nigeria –September 2008). The issues about behavior patterns that make MSM in United States and other countries of the world more likely to get HIV need to be confronted and the gay and bisexual men in all communities encouraged to protect each other.

Gay and bisexual men who are ready to quit may benefit from rehab and prevention programs similar to the rehab and prevention programs existing for all other behaviors associated with a higher possibility of deadly consequences, such as higher smoking habits and lung cancer, promiscuous female sex life with history of HPV and cervical cancer, higher consumption of alcohol and end stage liver disease of cirrhosis of the liver. The NGO, CBO, churches and other local agencies should consider the possibility of rehab programs and support for gay and bisexual men who wants to quit their sexual behavior that they perceive to be leading to HIV/AIDS infection and consequences of suffering from the disease complications and high health care cost before death. Rehab programs for gay and bisexual men needs to be explored to reduce the high burden of the HIV/AIDS. Some of them may be contemplating and ready to quit the gay and bisexual behavior to reduce their chances of getting HIV/AIDS.

Reading all these news articles reminds us that HIV will continue to be a problem in every country in the world. Therefore, mothers and fathers and families, which form the basic unit of every country, are encouraged to talk to their children, allow them to learn about STD/HIV infection and how to protect themselves and prevent getting STD/HIV infection. Parents should spend quality time with their children and young adults and help them to learn and adopt behaviors that will protect them and their would-be sex partners and marriage partners from STD/HIV. Then parents can team up with doctors and public health professionals to help teach and prevent the infectious diseases of STD/HIV. Such actions may prevent these adolescents and young adults from learning about STD/HIV from strangers in the street, anonymous sex partners, and people they meet on the Internet who will invariably get them into high-risk behaviors like men having sex with men, injection drug use and other drug abuse, multiple sex partners and sex escorts, and dependant behaviors of exchanging sex for money and drugs, which have been found to make such people become infected with STD/HIV and its associated suffering and early death.

Don't fail to change beliefs and practices to stop the HIV epidemic

The CDC released a report at HIV/AIDS daily news on the website http://cdc.gov/hiv/ on September 26, 2008, (CDC cited source:http://www.dpa.de/) that the UNAIDS conducted a survey in Beijing, Shanghai, Shenzhen, Wuhan, Zhengzhou, and Kunming cities of China and showing that mostly young Chinese do not understand how HIV is transmitted, while the stigma against those with the disease remains widespread. Among 6,000 people surveyed in the six cities, more than 48 percent believed HIV can be transmitted by mosquitoes, and 83 percent had never sought information about the disease. About 65 percent would be unwilling to live with an HIV positive person; 48 percent would not eat with someone who was HIV infected; and 41 percent would not work with a person who had HIV, the report said. About 32 percent agreed that people with HIV/AIDS "deserved their disease because of their sexual behavior or drug abuse." Of the 11 percent who said they had sex with someone who was not their regular partner in the previous six months, 42 percent had not used condoms. Just 19 percent thought they would use condoms with a new sex partner, and 30 percent did not know how to use condoms. However, 88 percent believed they were not at risk for HIV.

"We see that there are still many misconceptions around AIDS in the population, which contributed to stigma and discrimination," said Bernhard Schwartlaender, UNAIDS China coordinator. "But there are also worrying contradictions between knowledge and behavior. Though people know that HIV can be transmitted through unprotected sex, many still do not protect themselves with a condom when engaging in risk behavior."

HIV reports in China rose about 22 percent in 2007, according to the health ministry. About 45 percent of new cases were acquired heterosexually, and unprotected sex remains the "main mode for the spread of HIV," it said.

There is a similar misconception about HIV/AIDS all around the world, and it is time again for the community and the government to educate the people about HIV/AIDS. Mass media advertisement should be resumed as a very quick and efficient way of educating the public and the youth about HIV/AIDS. The acceptance and support of those who have HIV/AIDS by the community needs special attention. Such support to help take care of HIV/AIDS patients may facilitate open disclosure of HIV positive results to caring families, sex partners, and the community without fear of rejection.

A process of open disclosure of HIV status, sex behavior, and sexual risk behavior are all of public health importance to prevent and control infectious HIV and will also help people to openly discuss the risks involved in having sex and encourage them to seek protection from HIV-related risky behavior.

Public health workers and physicians should not assume that when people are diagnosed with HIV/AIDS they stop having sex. HIV/AIDS patients need to be asked about sex partners at every clinic visit.

They should talk about their safe sex history, and risk reduction must be discussed. STD screening should be done at regular six-month intervals and when symptomatic. When an HIV/AIDS positive patient has a sex partner, that person needs to be given the chance to test for HIV and practice safe sex to prevent a new HIV infection. It is not good enough to wait for the HIV/AIDS patient to get another STD before the sex partners are confidentially contacted for testing for both STDs and HIV. Active surveillance to reduce new HIV transmission knowingly and unknowing by working with HIV positive patients will be an important factor to control the HIV epidemic and must be taken serious.

People are allowed to choose the kind of sexual lifestyle they want, but when there is failure to communicate the facts of modifying a sexual lifestyle to prevent infectious disease that has no cure, the government will continuously have a burden of spending money and in some cases the scarce resources on many sick babies, children, and young adults, and the economy of the country would be affected by shrinking numbers of future active workers. The labor force of the community, villages, towns, cities, and the country will reduce. The situation could get serious especially in Africa and developing countries where there are very few doctors, nurses, and health personnel to take care of sick HIV/AIDS patients. Government must communicate STD/HIV risk information consistently to its citizens, support sound policies to prevent STD/HIV and keep the citizens healthy.

Many people have certain behaviors that can affect their health and life, but they find it difficult to stop those behaviors or make modifications to the behaviors to help them to stay healthy and avoid diseases like HIV/AIDS. Anybody who is not committed to only one sex partner who, in turn, is not committed to only that person has a chance of getting STD/HIV.

As a reminder, it will be to our great advantage to take a critical look at the excellent written testimony on HIV/AIDS incidence and prevention at a hearing on September 16, 2008, submitted to the U.S. House of Representative by Dr. David R. Holtgrave as a public health urgency. In the report, CDC's new estimates of HIV incidence suggest that, on average, a new HIV infection occurs every 9.5 minutes in the U.S. (Hall 2008). AIDS-related deaths occur roughly every thirty-three minutes. Racial and ethnic disparity burdens African American and Latino communities.

The incidence of HIV is rising among men who have sex with men (gays and bisexual men). HIV care and treatment cost $22,500 per year and approximately $275,000 for a lifetime treatment for the remaining years of an HIV positive patient (Holtgrave 2007, Chen 2006, Schackman 2006).

The HIV transmission rate, which is the number of new cases of HIV infection in a year divided by the number of people living with HIV in that year, gives us the sense of spread of HIV within a population in a geographic area. The HIV transmission rate dropped from 92.3 in 1980 to 6.6 in 1991 until 1997 with the use of HAART to treat HIV without a cure; the transmission rate increased to 7.5 per 100 HIV positive persons. By the application of evidenced-based intervention research to prevent and control HIV/AIDS, the estimated transmission rate is 5 per 100 HIV positive persons in 2006. This implies that 100 HIV positive patients infect 5 new persons with HIV per year. Global average transmission rate is 8.18 per 100 HIV positive patients (Kaiser Family Foundation 2008). But let us remember that in Africa and developing countries the transmission rate of HIV far exceeds the global average.

According to the report, the U.S. HIV prevention program has, up to 2006, prevented 362,000 people from getting HIV infection and over 3.3 million quality-adjusted years of life saved at a cost of $18.6 billion. The cost per prevention of a person getting HIV is $52,000 per lifetime, which is less than the cost of HIV care and treatment of $275,000 for one HIV positive person over the remaining lifetime after HIV infection.

From the report, it is obvious that prevention programs for HIV infection save money. At the same time it is clear that individual responsibility to make changes and modification to our so called "private sex life" to prevent HIV infection is a civic responsibility to save us and the family as well as the government and the country we love a lot of money that can be used to do other very important things to make our lives healthier and better.

In Africa and developing countries such medical expenses to treat HIV patients effectively will be an economic burden for governments and will cause undue suffering for the citizens, many of whom cannot even afford the cost of buying food to feed themselves in the setting of HIV infection and disease disability.

Diagnosis of STD in an HIV patient is a sign of transmission of HIV to sex partners. HIV prevention programs with innovations to do regular screening of HIV positive patients for STDs every six months and when symptomatic, and offering safe sex and HIV-related risk reduction health education and serial testing of all their sex partners for HIV infection, will be a viable option to pursue at the HIV clinics to effectively reduce the HIV transmission rate. The

HIV transmission rate is likely to be higher in HIV positive patients with new STD and having unprotected sex and especially, when the person is not taking HIV medications to reduce the viral load to undetectable level. In addition, sex partners of known sexually active HIV patients should be given the chance to know of their possible exposure to HIV infection and offered HIV health education and serial HIV screening tests for early diagnosis. This process of testing may prevent sex partners of known HIV patients who later may test HIV positive from unknowingly transmitting HIV infection to other sex partners in case there are multiple sexual relationships and when other HIV risk behaviors such as intravenous drug injections and drug use are involved.

The people who can identify themselves with the behaviors listed here have a higher chance of making a mistake and getting STDs, HIV, and AIDS. Such people are encouraged to make modifications to their sexual lifestyle and take STD/HIV prevention action seriously. Persons with these behaviors, beliefs, and practices and their sex partners have increased chance of getting STD/HIV infection:

1. Men who have sex with other men

2. Polygamous males and females and those who have more than one sex partner

3. Bisexual males and females

4. IV drug users and users of cocaine, alcohol, marijuana and other drugs that impair judgment

5. Sex for drugs, money, and other items and sex with commercial sex workers (prostitutes)

6. Sex with a person who has any of these behaviors and has been in jail or prison

7. Returning to old sex partners after so many months or years of separation or incarceration in prison without testing first for STD/HIV. Most sex partners who are not married cannot wait for their sex partners after separation due to travel and incarceration in jail or prison.

8. Sex with anonymous sex partners or pick up sex escorts and Internet sex partners especially sex partners met via Internet chat rooms

9. Sex with a new sex partner without testing for STD/HIV

10. Sex with someone who has a previous history of STDs like chlamydia, gonorrhea, syphilis, hepatitis B and C

11. Sex with a man who has a wife or a baby with another woman who is still receiving child support. If a person cannot be faithful with his wife or husband or previous girlfriend or boyfriend, then that person is less likely to be faithful to you.

12. Sex with a person who lies about previous sex life or refuses to faithfully discuss sex life or refuses to show evidence of negative STD/HIV test results. If a person lies about previous sex life or sex partners, he or she is more likely to lie about many other sex partners.

13. Sex with a homeless person especially when the person is a drug user or alcoholic

14. Sex with someone who refuses to test together with you for STD/HIV or show you results of an HIV test. When a

person loves and cares about a sex partner, testing together for STD/HIV and waiting to know the results together will not be a problem.

In all situations, remember to test your would-be sex partner for STD/HIV first before committing to a sexual relationship. In case a person has any of the high risk behaviors for STD/HIV as stated, the chance of getting HIV/AIDS is higher and therefore STD/HIV test counselors, doctors, nurses, STD/HIV epidemiologist and disease intervention specialist and other STD/HIV workers involved in direct patient care must make such persons aware of such behaviors and motivate them to initiate early behavior modifications and changes to prevent coming into contact with STD/HIV infection. As a reminder, those who already have HIV infection and are aware of their test results, please do no harm. Such persons are to inform their doctors, dentist, and sex partners of their HIV positive test results so that they can help take care of the HIV positive patients and protect themselves and other people from HIV infection. HIV positive patients should not share needles, syringes, and razors and cannot donate blood, blood products, and body organs. They should use condoms always.

HIV/AIDS continues to be a major public health problem all over the world especially among men who have sex with men, low socioeconomic groups in the developed countries, and in Africa and developing countries even after twenty-five years of the beginning of the disease epidemic. There is still no cure and no vaccine.

Cultural norms, values, beliefs, and practices increase the chance of STD/HIV infection in young women and men who have sex with men. Factors such as high fertility rate, lack of effective prevention to protect women, and perinatal HIV medication for treatment of pregnant women and babies as well as lack of formula feeding and the desire of HIV positive mothers to continue to breastfeed because of lack of funds to buy sufficient formula feeds, milk, and milk products to feed their babies will continue to increase the chance of babies getting HIV infection from their HIV positive mothers especially in Africa unless policies are made to solve these problems.

There is a potential trend of increasing vertical transmission of HIV infection from pregnant mothers to babies especially in Africa and developing countries as more men continue to have multiple sex partners. That increases the chances of more young women getting infected with STD and HIV/AIDS. However there is hope if men all over the world will protect themselves and then protect women. And also, medical research can be made accessible to Africa and developing countries to bridge the gaps of beliefs and cultural practices and reverse the trend of the STD/HIV epidemic.

Men and women should do everything possible to modify and adopt behaviors that will make them stay married. Men who decide not to marry but decide to have sexual relationships outside marriage should use condoms properly to protect themselves and the women. By doing so, they will protect babies too from STD and HIV/AIDS. Women should always remind men to be faithful as they themselves remain faithful to men. If they choose to have sex before marriage, they must make sure that the men test for STD/HIV, negotiate for consistent and proper use of condoms to protect them since the best way to avoid getting deadly diseases that have no cure and no vaccine like HIV/AIDS is to avoid coming into contact with the germ or virus that causes the infection and the disease complications.

Only the families, communities, nations, and people that initiate and maintain bold measures and behaviors that will make people avoid coming into contact with STD/HIV can survive and control the epidemic of HIV/AIDS and live a healthy life. HIV is a very smart virus, changing and hiding in the body most of the time to avoid being killed by the body's immune system and medications.

Doctors and other health workers involved in patient care must endeavor to ask for consent to help their patients to adopt healthy sexual lifestyles to avoid STD/HIV. Teachers, parents, and politicians should not feel shy or avoid their responsibility of discussing the prevention of infectious diseases like STD/HIV with their students, children, and citizens. Policymakers should not be afraid to do open and continuous advertisement and advocate to encourage people to adopt healthy sexual lifestyles to avoid coming into contact with and spreading infectious and deadly STDs like HIV and hepatitis B and C. Individuals must read and fill knowledge gaps about STD/HIV prevention.

Let us encourage new ideas in HIV medical research and interventional research in STD/HIV. Hopefully, one day, a cure and a vaccine for HIV infection could be found. But until then, STD/HIV prevention action is absolutely necessary. Let's protect each other and avoid unnecessary suffering and early death from infectious diseases like STD/HIV.

References

Avert 2001. AIDS in Africa. http://www.avert.org/aafrica.htm.

Braunwald, E. et al. *Harrison's Principles of Internal Medicine.* 15th edition. McGraw Hill, 2001, pp. 1852, 1873–1891.

Bartlett, J.G. et al. in the book 2000-2001 Medical Management of HIV infection.

Bryson, Y.J. 1996. Perinatal HIV-1 transmission: Recent advances and therapeutic intervention. *AIDS* 10 (Suppl. 3): S33–S42.

Bulterys, M. and P. Le Page. 1998. Mother-to-child transmission of HIV. *Current Opinions in Paediatrics* 10 (2): 143–150.

Centers for Disease Control and Prevention. Healthy Youth! Sexual Risk Behaviors. http://www.cdc.gov/HealthyYouth/sexualbehaviors/index.htm.

Centers for Disease Control and Prevention. HIV/AIDS and African Americans. http://www.cdc.gov/hiv/topics/aa/index.htm.

Centers for Disease Control and Prevention. HIV/AIDS and Men Who Have Sex with Men (MSM). http://www.cdc.gov/hiv/topics/msm/index.htm.

Centers for Disease Control and Prevention. 2006. Investigation of a New Diagnosis of Multiple-Resistant, Dual-Tropic HIV-1 Infection–New York City, 2005. *MMWR,* July 28, 2006: 55(29).

Centers for Disease Control and Prevention. 2008. Subpopulation Estimates from the HIV Incidence Surveillance System–United States, 2006. *MMWR,* September 12, 2008: 57(36): 985–989.

Chen, R.Y. et al. 2006. Distribution of health care expenditure for HIV-infected patients. *Clin Infect Dis.* 42: 1003–1010.

Connor, E.M., et al. 1994. Reduction of maternal-infant transmission of Human Immunodeficiency Virus type 1 with zidovudine treatment. *New England Journal of Medicine,* 331:1173–1180.

French, P.P. et al. 2003. Use-effectiveness of the female versus male condom in preventing sexually transmitted disease in women. *Sex Transmit Dis* 30:433–439.

Garcia, P.M. et al. 1999. Maternal levels of plasma Human Immunodeficiency

Virus type 1 RNA and the risk of perinatal transmission. *New England Journal of Medicine* 341: 394–402.

Guay, L.A., et al. 1999. Intrapartum and neonatal single dose Nevirapine compared with zidovudine for prevention of mother-to-child-transmission of HIV-1 in Kampala, Uganda, HIVNET012 Randomized Trial. *Lancet* 354: 795–802.

Hall, H. et al. 2008. Estimation of HIV incidence in United States. *JAMA* 300:(5):520–529.

Hogen Woning C.J.A. et al. 2003. Condom use promotes regression of cervical intraepithelial neoplasia and clearance of human papilloma virus. A randomized clinical trial. *Int J Cancer* 107: 811–816.

Holmes, K.K. et al. 2004. Effectiveness of condoms in preventing sexually transmitted infections. *Bull World Health Organ.* 82:454–461.

Holtgrave, D.R. 2007. Cost and Consequences of the US Centers for Disease Control and Prevention's recommendations for opt-out HIV testing. *Plos Med.* 4(6):1011–1018.

Joint United Nations Programme on HIV/AIDS (UNAIDS) & World Health Organization (WHO). 2002. *AIDS Epidemic Update: December 2002.* http://www.unaids.org.

Kaiser Family Foundation. HIV/AIDS Policy Fact Sheet. July 2008.

Kamwenda F, et al. 1996. Decreasing incidence of gonorrhea- and chlamydia-associated acute pelvic inflammatory disease: A 25-year study from urban areas of central Sweden. *Sex Transmit Dis* 23:384–391.

Kimberly A.W. and M.B. Stuart MB. 2006. Prevention Methods for STD/HIV, Male Condoms. Sexually Transmitted Diseases Treatment Guidelines, 2006. Division of STD Prevention, National Center for HIV, Viral Hepatitis, STDs and Tuberculosis Prevention. *Morbidity and Mortality Weekly Report.* August 4, 2006 (55): No. RR-11:4.

Kuhn, L. et al. 2008. Effects of Early, Abrupt Weaning for HIV-free Survival of Children in Zambia. *New England Journal of Medicine*, June 4.

Kumwenda, N. I. et al. 2008. Extended Antiretroviral Prophylaxis to Reduce Breast-Milk HIV-1 Transmission. *New England Journal of Medicine* June 4.

MacPhail, C. et al. 2002. Relative Risk of HIV Infection Among Young Men and Women in a South African Township. *J of STD AIDS*.

Manhart, L.E. and L.A. Koutsky. 2002. Do condoms prevent genital HPV infection, external genital warts, or cervical neoplasia? A meta-analysis. *Sexually Transmitted Diseases* 29:725–735.

Morbidity and Mortality Weekly Report (*MMWR*). Recommendations and Reports. August 4, 2006/vol. 55/No. RR-11: 16, 42–44, 71.

National Institutes of Health. National Institute of Allergy and Infectious Diseases. http://www.niaid.nih.gov.

Nduati, R. et al. 2000. Effect of breastfeeding and formula feeding on transmission of HIV-1: A randomized clinical trial. *Journal of the American Medical Association* 283: 1167–1174.

Ness, R.B. et al. 2004. Condom use and the risk of recurrent pelvic inflammatory disease, chronic pelvic pain, or infertility following an episode of pelvic inflammatory disease. *Am J Public Health* 94:1327–1329.

Palella FJ Jr, et al. 1998. Declining morbidity and mortality among patients with advanced human immunodeficiency virus infection. New England Journal of Medicine; 338:853-860.

Public Health Service Task Force. Recommendations for use of antiretroviral drugs in pregnant HIV-1 infected women for maternal health and interventions to reduce perinatal HIV-1 transmission in the United States. Rockville, MD: U.S. Department of Health and Human Services, National Institutes of Health, Health Resources and Services Administration; 2005. http://www.aidsinfo.nih.gov.

Ramos, A.J.T. et al. 2000. Estimate of HIV-1 infection prevalence in pregnant women and effectiveness of zidovudine administered during pregnancy in the prevention of vertical transmission. *Medical Clinics (Barcelona)* 114 (8): 286–291.

Romanowski B, et al. 2003. Valtrex HS230017 Study Group, Roberts JN. Patients preference of valacyclovir once-daily suppressive therapy versus twice daily episodic therapy for recurrent genital herpes: a randomized study. *Sex Transmit Dis* 30:226–231.

Sands, M. et al 2007. DOT data reference. Duval County Health Department. Jacksonville, Florida.

Schackman, B.R. et al. 2006. The lifetime costs of current human immunodeficiency virus care in the United States. *Med Care* 44(11):990–997.

Scholes D. et al. 1996. Prevention of pelvic inflammatory disease by screening for cervical chlamydia infection. *New England Journal of Medicine* 334:1362–1366.

Sharp, Paul M. and Beatrice H. Hahn. 2008. AIDS: Prehistory of HIV-1. *Nature* 455, 605-606.

Stinger, J.S.A. and S.H. Bermund. 1999. Prevention of mother-to-infant transmission of HIV-1. *Current Opinions in Obstetrics and Gynecology* 11: 427–434.

Sweat, M. et al. 2001. Cost effectiveness of a brief video-based HIV intervention for African American and Latino Sexually Transmitted Disease Clinic Clients. *AIDS*. 15:781–787.

Tabi, M.M. and S. Frimpong. 2003. HIV infection of women in African countries. *2003 International Council of Nurses*: 242–250.

UNAIDS, Report on the Global AIDS Epidemic, 2004

U.S. Preventive Services Task Force. 2001. Screening for chlamydia infection recommendations and rationale. *Am J Prev Med* 20 (Suppl 3):90–94.

Valdisseri et al. in book, Nature Medicine 2003.

Wald, A. et al. 2001. Effect of condom on reducing the transmission of herpes simplex virus type 2 from men to women. *JAMA* 27:285:3100–3106.

Wald, A. et al. 2005. The relationship between condom use and herpes simplex virus acquisition. *Ann Intern Medicine* 143:707–713.

Washington Manual of Medical Therapeutics. 2001. 30th edition: 382–383.

Winer, R et al. 2006. Consistent condom use from time of first vaginal intercourse and the risk of genital human papilloma virus infection in young women. *New England Journal of Medicine* 354:2645–2654.

World Development Indicators Database. 2000. http://www.worldbank.org/html/extdr/regions.htm.

World Health Organization, Department of HIV/AIDS, "Training Guide for HIV Prevention Outreach to Injecting Drug Users," 2003, http://www.emro.who.int/aiecf/web6.pdf.

About the Author

Dr. Samuel Frimpong, MD, MPH, is an internal medicine specialist and a CDC-trained disease intervention specialist for STD and HIV infections. He also has HIV surveillance certification from the Florida Health Department Bureau of HIV/AIDS. He works at the Duval County Health Department HIV and STD clinics in Jacksonville, Florida. He is a human services program specialist for the AIDS program and does HIV risk reduction intervention consultation for physicians at both the HIV and STD clinics.

Dr. Frimpong received his initial medical training from the University of Ghana Medical School in Accra, Ghana, West Africa, where he graduated in 1994. He worked at the Korle-bu teaching hospital in Accra as a physician prior to immigrating to the United States for further training in internal medicine and public health. He is a naturalized citizen of the U.S.

Dr. Frimpong has worked in the public health sector and in hospital settings for the past fourteen years. In the U.S. he pursued a career in public health and internal medicine at the University of Alabama School of Public Health at Birmingham and the Medical College of Georgia, respectively.

His training in medicine, and master's degree in public health and epidemiology and international health, has given him the passion to work with people from different backgrounds and behaviors. He has worked with patients in hospitals, mental health settings, and with troubled inmates in prisons, STD/HIV patients, and their sex partners in the community.

Prior to working at the STD and HIV clinics, he spent three years doing STD/HIV contact investigation and screening tests in the city of Jacksonville and helped people with STD and HIV to get treatment. He facilitated confidential testing and treatment of sex partners for STD/HIV infections. He continues to work with the Health Planning Council of Northeast Florida on weekends and helps to mobilize the community for STD/HIV screening and prevention education.

On July 30, 2008, Dr. Frimpong received the Tommy Chandler Award for his outstanding work in STD prevention from the Florida Public Health Association. The award states: *The Florida Department of Health Bureau of STD Prevention and Control is pleased to award the 6th Annual Tommy Chandler Outstanding Disease Intervention Specialist Award to Samuel Frimpong for his outstanding contributions to the Area four STD Prevention Program and the Bureau of STD Prevention and Control.* In February 2009, he received Leadership Award for Disease Control from the Duval County Health Department. The award citation: *This Is To Certify That Samuel Frimpong Is Hereby Awarded*

This Certificate of Special Recognition For Leadership Award For Disease Control.

Dr. Frimpong worked with a team of seven disease intervention specialists of the Duval County Health Department, Division of Communicable Diseases STD Field Operations Unit, that received the Senior Management Award 2007 and Promising Program Award 2007 for using the innovative field directly observed therapy (DOT) for chlamydia and gonorrhea to control and reduce the number of cases of chlamydia and gonorrhea in Jacksonville for the period of 2005 to 2007. He exceeded the State of Florida Health Department standard for syphilis and HIV sex partner contact investigation index in 2007.

He serves as an active member of the First Coast Community AIDS Prevention Partnership (FCCAPP) of Northeast Florida and the World AIDS Day Planning Committee in Jacksonville, Florida.

One of Dr. Frimpong's goals is to help people especially the youth and young adults age 15–24 all over the world to increase their knowledge about STD/HIV infection and prevention and motivate them to take action to protect themselves from STD/HIV.

Dr. Frimpong began his medical residency internship at the Good Samaritan Hospital in Baltimore, Maryland. During that period, he had the opportunity to do infectious disease clinical electives at the Johns Hopkins University Hospital in 2000, which furthered his understanding of the complexities of HIV structural changes and its ability to invade the body's immune system as well as the difficulties associated with vaccine production because of such structural changes. It became obvious to him that it will take a longer-than-expected time to produce a vaccine to prevent HIV infection and that behavior modification to avoid contact with HIV infection will be the key to prevent and control HIV infection until a vaccine is found.

In that year, he was part of a team of physicians that managed patients with AIDS. These patients did not know they had HIV infection until they came to the hospital. They were very sick with opportunistic infections of HIV that had spread throughout their bodies. They suffered significantly before getting better and eventually left to go home. Many patients with such late presentation of HIV infections die in other parts of the world where HIV medical care is not very good and even in developed countries like United States where HIV medical treatment without cure is available.

Together with his team of physicians at Good Samaritan Hospital, Dr. Frimpong presented a clinical poster of one of such late diagnosis of opportunistic infections known as disseminated histoplasmosis in an HIV patient at a clinical scientific conference of medical resident physicians called Associate of America College of Physicians/American Society for Internal Medicine (ACP-ASIM) conference in 2000 at Baltimore.

He made a clinical poster presentation about leukemia called Smoldering Myeloma Evolving During Treatment of Chronic Myelogenous Leukemia (CML) with Imatinib Mesylate at the Associate ACP-ASIM conference in Atlanta 2002, while in the final year of internal medicine resident training at the Medical College of Georgia, Augusta, Georgia. He received an award of a medal from the Medical College of Georgia Internal Medicine Residency Program for that clinical poster presentation.

Dr. Frimpong enjoys helping people to get treatment for diseases and taking action to prevent diseases. He likes writing, vigilant clinical observations, and contributing to medical and public health knowledge.

In 2003, Dr. Frimpong co-authored with Marian M. Tabi, RN, PhD, MPH, Assistant Professor of Nursing at the Georgia Southern University in Statesboro, Georgia, a journal article, HIV Infection of Women in African Countries, published in the *2003 International Council of Nurses, International Nursing Review.* He has always been concerned about the negative consequences of HIV/AIDS on the family when women and children get HIV infection, when children become orphans early in life and miss the opportunity to achieve their full potential because of HIV infection.

He is a member of the Florida Public Health Association, American Public Health Association, Global Health Council, associate member of American College of Physician and American Society of Internal Medicine (ACP-ASIM), Ghana Medical Association, and Ghana Medical and Dental Council.

Index

treatment of, 127–133

    See also HIV (human immunodeficiency virus)

AIDS Drug Assistance Program (ADAP), xxv

anal abscess, 16

anal sex, 14–16, 201–202

anonymous sex partners, xi, 13, 21, 24, 26, 30, 35, 225

ATBC prevention, 19, 32, 35, 52, 55, 63–64, 116

B

baby's dad, 22, 23

baby's mother, 22

Bangladesh, 18

behavior modification, 11, 19–21, 28, 36–37, 197, 201–202, 218, 227

    See also prevention action plan

behaviors, high-risk, xxi, xxiii, 11, 12–18, 19–21, 29, 172–175, 224–226

beliefs, 226

Bible quotes, 160–169

bisexual behavior, 26, 29, 53–54, 153, 154, 173, 201, 215–218

Bletcher, Mark, 190

blood transfusions, 114, 116, 137

Botswana, xxv, 57, 177, 199

bottle feeding, 44–46, 113, 178, 186–187, 227

Brazil, xxviii, 58

breastfeeding, 42, 44, 113, 116, 177–178, 185–186, 227

bulbourethral glands, 8

Bush, George W., xxv

C
Cameroon, 141, 144, 148
cancer
  of the anus, 16
  of the cervix, 26, 48, 101, 103–104, 115
  Kaposi's sarcoma, 16, 114, 115, 119
  of the liver, 96
  lymphoma, 115, 119
candida infections, 115, 118, 120, 131
Caribbean, xxvii, xxv
CD4 counts, 131–133, 134, 193–194
Centers for Disease Control and Prevention (CDC),
    xxii, 15, 17, 50-56, 60
cervical cancer, 26, 48, 101, 103–104, 115
cervix, 2–4, 9, 71
chancroid, 65, 66, 85–86
chiefs, 152
chimpanzees, 133, 134, 142, 144, 146, 148
China, xxviii, 219–220
chlamydia, 14, 18, 38, 49–50, 65, 66, 70, 71–74
church, teachings of, 152, 212–213, 218
  See also Bible quotes
cirrhosis, 96
community-based organization (CBO), 57, 154, 186,
    218
community leaders, 186
condom usage, 12, 16, 18–19, 20, 39, 48, 63, 150–
    151
condylomata acuminata, 66, 101–107

epithelial cells, 2
Epstein Barr virus, 119
Estonia, 17
Ethiopia, xxv

F
fallopian tubes, xix–xx, 2–4, 5–6, 9, 14, 69, 71
Fauci, Anthony, 194
fertility, fertility rate, 45, 177, 226
fertilization, 4, 9
fimbriae, 4
formula feeding, 44–46, 113, 178, 186–187, 227

G
Gardasil, 26, 101, 106–107
genital herpes, 66, 98–100
genital warts, 16, 48, 66, 101–107, 121
Ghana, 138, 176
gonorrhea, 14, 18, 38, 49–50, 65, 66, 67–71
government, 152, 154, 179, 186, 221
granuloma inguinale, 65, 66, 87–88
Guyana, xxv

H
HAART (highly active antiretroviral therapy), 12, 36,
        52, 58, 113, 114, 115, 127–133
Hahn, Beatrice H., 143–145
Haiti, xxv, xxvii
Health behavior scientist, 32
Health workers, 228
hemophilia, 93, 114

Leopoldville, 139–149
leptospirosis, 136
Lesotho, 177
Lyme disease, 136
lymphogranuloma venerum (LGV), 65, 66, 88–89
lymphoma, 115, 119

M
Manuel, Trevor, 190
Mbeki, Thabo, 188, 189
menses. *See* menstrual cycle
menstrual cycle, 4, 121
men who have sex with men (MSM), 13, 15–16, 18,
      20–21, 53-54, 216-217
mental health, 34
Mexico, xxvii
monogamy, xxi–xxii, xxx, 19, 28, 55
monogamous relationship, 28, 37
mother-child transmission. *See* vertical transmission
Motlante, Kgalema, 189
Mozambique, xxv
Multiple simultaneous sex partners, 30
Myanmar, 17

N
Namibia, xxv
nevirapine, 42–43, 45, 116, 157, 186, 190
new sex partner syndrome, 21–22, 26, 30
Nigeria, xxv, xxvi, 217
non-governmental organization (NGO), 57, 154,
      179, 185-186, 218

Nurses, 32, 179, 184, 221

O
occupational exposure, 116, 152, 195
old sex partner syndrome, 21–22, 26, 28, 30
oocytes, 4
oral sex, 14–15, 202
orchitis, 10, 69
ovaries, 2–4, 6

P
Pap smears, xix, 101, 106
parasites, 67, 107–112
parents, 228
parentheral transmission, 116
Partnership for Health, 151
Paul M. Sharp, 145
pediculosis pubis, 66, 67, 109–110
pelvic abscess, 5, 69
pelvic inflammatory disease (PID), 5, 14, 71, 72,
        73–74
pelvic peritonitis, 69
penis, 8–9
PEPFAR (President's Emergency Plan for AIDS
        Relief), xxv–xxvii, xxix, 46, 58
pneumocyctis carinii pneumonia (PCP), 114, 115,
        131
pneumonia, 114, 115, 118
policymakers, 152, 178
Political will, 113

Russian Federation, xxviii, 17, 18, 19
Rwanda, xxv
Rwanda Zambia HIV research group (RZHRG), 60
Ryan White Care Act, xxiv–xxv, 58

S
SAFE (Serostatus Approach to Fighting the HIV
     Epidemic), 150
salpingitis, 5
SARS (severe acute respiratory syndrome), 56, 136
scabies, 66, 67, 110–112, 121
Schwartlaender, Bernhard, 220
secretory glands, 8
semen, 9
seminal vesicles, 9
Senegal, 57
septic abortions, 6–7
sex education, 206–208, 209–210
sex partners, 11, 33, 14
sex escorts, 36
sexual risk behaviors, xxi, xxiii, 11, 12–18, 19–21,
     29, 172–175, 224–226
shingles, 115, 121
sickle cell anemia, 93, 137
social conservatism, 209
socio-economic burdens, xxix, 58
South Africa, xxvi–xxvii, 177, 187–191
Southern AIDS Coalition (SAC), 209
sperm, 8–9
STDs (sexually transmitted diseases)
   and increased risk for HIV, 14, 117

tubal stricture, 5
tuberculosis (TB), 115, 131
tubo-ovarian abscess, 6, 69

U
Uganda, xxv, 50, 57
urine retention, 9
United States Agency for International Development
    (USAID), xxv
United States (U.S.), xxiv, xxv, 15, 134, 159, 204
  Alaska, 206
  California, 135, 213, 216
  District of Columbia, 215
  Florida, 200, 209
  Michigan, 202
  New York, 17, 114, 134-135, 216
  Washington, DC, 193, 217
Ukraine, 17
United Kingdom, 17
uterus, 2–4, 5–6, 9, 71

V
vagina, 2–4, 9
values, 226
vertical transmission, 18, 41–46, 58–59, 113, 116,
    177–178, 183–188, 227
viral loads, 131–133, 134, 193–194
Vietnam, 57
Voices for Planned Parenthood (VOX), 206
VOICES/VOCES, 130, 150–151